IN OUR BACKYARD

HUMAN TRAFFICKING

IN AMERICA

AND WHAT WE CAN

DO TO STOP IT

NITA BELLES

BakerBooks

a division of Baker Publishing Group
Grand Rapids, Michigan

© 2015 by Nita Belles

Published by Baker Books
a division of Baker Publishing Group
P.O. Box 6287, Grand Rapids, MI 49516-6287
www.bakerbooks.com

Printed in the United States of America

Library of Congress Cataloging-in-Publication Data is on file at the Library of Congress, Washington, DC.

ISBN 978-0-8010-1857-2

Scripture quotations are from the Holy Bible, New International Version®. NIV®. Copyright © 1973, 1978, 1984, 2011 by Biblica, Inc.™ Used by permission of Zondervan. All rights reserved worldwide. www.zondervan.com

Published in association with Ambassador Literary Agency, Nashville, TN.

While all the human trafficking incidents described in this book are true, stories have occasionally been dramatized to convey the tragedy of human trafficking on a personal level. In addition, names and other identifying characteristics have been changed in some instances to protect victims' privacy and safety.

Whenever a name has been changed to protect identity, an asterisk (*) follows the name when it first appears. Out of respect, all victims' statements have been quoted verbatim. The author chose not to correct or draw attention to any grammatical errors made by those whose native language is not English.

Some of the material contained in this book is for mature audiences.

15   16   17   18   19   20   21   7   6   5   4   3   2   1

This book is dedicated to all the precious ones being used as modern-day slaves, to those of you who are sleeping in doorways or on the floors of garages, utility rooms, warehouses, crowded houses and apartments, and other places you never wanted to be. It's for those of you who have given up hope of finding help and those of you with a shred of hope left.

It comes with a message that you are loved—by people you've given up on, by a God who loves you in the midst of your circumstances—and with a message that many of us who care are on the move. We are committed to doing what we can and to petitioning God on your behalf for the rest. Yes, you are loved. Believe it.

Contents

Acknowledgments

After many months and even years of hard work, I would like to thank numerous people who have helped make this book possible. Thanks to the many survivors, government officials, law enforcement personnel, ex-perpetrators, and those who work with victims in rescue and recovery for your time and your willingness to be vulnerable in order to help others by sharing from your lives.

Thanks to my family for putting up with my being endlessly busy and preoccupied with this work. A *huge* thanks to my wonderful husband, Dan; without his unending support, his long days and nights of working with me on this issue, and his patience and love, I couldn't have written this book and couldn't do what I do each day.

Most of all, I give thanks to God.

These three remain: faith, hope and love. But the greatest of these is love. (1 Cor. 13:13)

May this book help to demonstrate that love in helping to end the atrocity of modern slavery.

Preface

We have only begun to scratch the surface in the fight against human trafficking. If there were only one soul still being trafficked, our fight against this atrocity would continue, but the ugly truth is that there are millions. We have much more work remaining.

This book is a resource to help regular citizens understand what human trafficking is, how to recognize it, and what to do if they see it. Human trafficking exists in every state and nearly every city. If you look hard enough, you'll even find it in our nation's small towns and in the countryside. In short, it's *in our backyard*. And we can all help stop this atrocity.

I live in a beautiful rural area. Our region consists of small, sleepy western towns, cities, and farming communities, with some of the seemingly safest streets in the country. Tourism abounds here, with 315 days of sunshine a year, wide-open spaces, rivers, lakes, mountains, and air that smells so good it should be bottled. Not surprisingly, this area attracts conventions and other gatherings, as well as wealthy (some *very* wealthy) individuals looking for upscale and resort living. If human trafficking can happen in my hometown, it can and does happen anywhere. No community is immune.

I began to study human trafficking while working on my master's degree in 2005. The stories I uncovered were the most tragic I had ever known. "What can I do?" I asked. The answer that came surprised me: "Write a book about human trafficking."

I had never written a book before—my gifts seemed to be in teaching, training, networking, motivating, and caring deeply about individuals. Doing those things came easily to me. By contrast, writing this book was very difficult. I felt I was being asked to do something not impossible but well out of my comfort zone.

My hope is that this book will help save some child, some young woman, some young man, as it encourages all of us to love as we would want to be loved in this fight against human trafficking and beyond. I've written stories I've seen and heard, stories that have broken my heart and, I suspect, will break yours as well.

It certainly broke my heart when I learned about what was happening in other places around the globe. But when I understood what was happening here in America, in this country where I live and which I dearly love, I knew this is where I was called to make a difference. I have lived my entire life here and never realized until 2006 that slavery still exists on US soil. I had to do something.

What do I have to offer the victims and survivors of modern slavery? While I'm often described as an expert on this subject, I am still learning every day. My best teachers, and the ones I respect beyond words, are those who have survived and are surviving this atrocity.

None of us can be all things to all people. I wouldn't last long kicking down brothel doors and grabbing pimps by the back of the neck with a "Listen here, young man!" But most of us can tell people about human trafficking, sit with a victim and listen to him or her, guide victims to services to help in their recovery, work to improve legislation, call the authorities when we see something that looks suspiciously like human trafficking, and network with anti-trafficking organizations and agencies. By doing these things, we can take a stand and might even save lives in our own community.

This book is not intended to be an all-inclusive look at modern slavery in the United States, but rather a sampling to inspire you to uncover more truths about this outrage for yourself. Although I mention the work of many organizations, I have intentionally not endorsed specific anti-trafficking organizations. Instead, once you realize how pervasive this tragedy of human trafficking is, I encourage you to get behind one or more of the many anti-trafficking groups, especially in your own backyard, and support it as a volunteer or by financial donations.

I must admit I hesitated to share some reports of victims' experiences that are so horrific I feared you might be tempted to doubt them. But to give you the full scope of what's really happening in our country, I have included a number of them anyway. Unfortunately, the truth is sometimes worse than what you might imagine.

1

Modern Slavery

It's Everywhere

All that is necessary for the triumph of evil is that good men [or women] do nothing.

—Edmund Burke

Sarah* carefully navigated the early-morning traffic to school in "Betsy," a silver 2003 Honda Accord with black leather seats and bright chrome wheels, which her parents had given her for her sixteenth birthday. Two weeks earlier, her parents had thrown her a sweet-sixteen birthday party with pizza and prizes at church after youth group. All her closest friends had come and watched as she was presented with "Betsy." A big sign on the windshield read "HAPPY BIRTHDAY SARE-BEAR!" Sare-Bear was her parents' endearing name for her and a reminder of how special she was to them.

The present, however, had come with conditions. Her upper-middle-class parents had given her just two months to get a job to pay for Betsy's gas and insurance. And despite Sarah's 4.0 GPA, her new car also came with a curfew and the insistence from her parents that they know where she was and who she was with at all times.

The morning had not started off well. Sarah hated arguing with her mom, but lately her parents' rules had been getting under her skin. "With privilege comes responsibility," they said. But now they were even telling her what she could and couldn't wear. Just last week she had bought a shirt from Abercrombie that her mom made her return because it was "too tight and too low." She didn't really want to be a bad girl; she just wanted to fit in with what the other kids were wearing. Besides, she really liked that shirt!

As she pulled into the school parking lot, she saw her new friend Maggie* wearing the exact shirt she'd been forced to return. Maggie not only had nice clothes, but she had all the freedom she wanted. This was high school after all, the time to have fun. Why couldn't her parents be more like Maggie's?

"Hey, Sarah!" Maggie was always so happy to see her and seemed truly friendly. "How was your weekend?"

"It was good. My family went to the beach. I really like your shirt! I actually bought that shirt, but my mom made me return it."

"Why? Was there something wrong with it?"

"No, my parents thought it was too tight. Maybe I should have bought a bigger size." In front of Maggie, Sarah always felt like she had to make excuses for her parents' rules.

"That's how these are supposed to be worn. Hey, I'll give you mine tomorrow. I'm going to the mall tonight, and I'll get myself something new. Besides, I think this is a better color for you than for me. It will look so cute on you."

"Maggie, you don't have to do that. Besides, my mom would freak out if she saw me wearing that after she made me take it back."

"Why would you need to tell her? Just leave it in your locker here at school."

Before Sarah could say anything, Maggie continued. "Your parents seem really strict. I'm trusted to make my own rules. I don't have curfews. I do what I want, when I want to do it."

That sounded good to Sarah, especially after the way she and her parents had been butting heads lately. They said she was rebellious, but how could she not be? They didn't seem to understand her or her needs. They had no idea what it was like to be a teenager today.

The next day, Maggie came not only with the coveted shirt but with another one as well. "Here's the shirt I promised, along with this other one I thought would look so sweet on you. It will show off your curves. If you've got it, flaunt it!" They both laughed.

"I can't take both of these. I don't know how I could possibly pay you back," Sarah said. She had been applying for jobs at all the clothing stores in the mall as well as at all the fast-food places, but no one seemed to be hiring.

"Don't worry about it." Maggie winked at her. "There's more where that came from. Let's hurry before we're late for history."

Sarah changed into the new shirt after first period and ate lunch with Maggie that day.

"Doesn't it feel good to wear what *you* want to wear? You look so pretty in that shirt! You're doing the right thing by following your heart."

Their friendship grew. Maggie was so at ease with herself, a trait Sarah admired.

And she loved how Maggie made her laugh. Even though her jokes were a little crude, Maggie was so much fun and her life seemed so much more exciting than Sarah's. Before long, Sarah confided in Maggie about her unsuccessful job search.

"I need to get a job to pay for insurance and gas for my car. Plus, I want to be able to buy some clothes to keep at school so my parents can't forbid them," she said with a sigh.

"Hey, the work I do is really easy. I can totally set you up," Maggie offered. "All you have to do is go on a date with this guy. You'll have to make out a little, but it won't be a big deal. And I can get you forty bucks for it, which should cover your gas for the week."

"Who is the guy?"

"No one we know. He's older and just a little lonely. You just have to pretend you really like him for a couple of hours. It's easy money!"

Forty bucks to go out on a date? That sounded good to Sarah. Her parents would think she was at the school football game, and she could still make her curfew. The guy was in his twenties and she'd only be with him for a short time. Besides, the idea that her parents would think she was at the game while she was earning some quick cash seemed exciting.

Slippery Slope

The date didn't quite go as advertised. The guy demanded more than just making out. Sarah was uncomfortable at first, but it wasn't like she had sex with him. He only pushed to get to "second base," as the girls at school would say.

As promised, Maggie was waiting for Sarah after the date. She soothed her friend's concerns, and they had time to grab a Coke before Sarah had to go home. Maggie mixed some vodka in hers but Sarah declined. The date was one thing, but she knew better than to drink and drive. As they chatted, Maggie shared her weekend plans, which included not just one date but two, and with different men no less. How Sarah envied her newfound friend!

Sarah, however, had no idea Maggie wasn't just a friend. She was actually what is known in sex trafficking as a "bottom b–tch." In a pimp's "stable" (the group of girls that he sells), there is continuous competition to be his favorite. The "bottom" is the most loyal and has a higher status both with him and within the stable. She can do many things the other girls can't, such as arrange dates for the other girls, collect money, train and discipline other girls, and recruit; however, she still has a monetary quota to meet by having her own prostituted dates. Befriending Sarah was just part of Maggie's job.

Sarah's weekend crawled by. Comparing Maggie's life to hers made hers seem even more boring. Sarah felt a little conflicted about what she had done on Friday, but at least she wasn't a "square," to use Maggie's terminology, like some of the other girls she knew from church. Sarah wouldn't find out until later that the word *square* is used in sex-trafficking circles to define anyone not involved in prostitution or what is more likely than not *forced* prostitution.

At school Monday morning, Maggie said that Sarah had really been a hit with her Friday date, and he wanted to get together with her again. They arranged for Sarah to meet him after school that Wednesday.

"You're so exciting to me," the man told sixteen-year-old Sarah.

His words pleased her and made her feel like a real woman. She agreed to drive up to the butte in his car to make out again. This time she was more comfortable. She really enjoyed the fact that her parents had *no* idea where she was and what she was doing.

Over the weeks that followed, Maggie and Sarah became better friends, and Sarah continued to go on occasional arranged dates. She could now afford insurance and gas for her car, had new clothes, and was leading a life as exciting as Maggie's. Besides, the lie she had told her parents about her new job was buying her extra time away from home. The increased fighting with her parents was unfortunate but worth it because, in addition to her new job, Sarah had a new romance.

Maggie had introduced Sarah to her friend Ace.* They were now secretly boyfriend and girlfriend. Sarah thought about him constantly. She was in love for the first time in her life, and he seemed to adore her. He had introduced her to sex and loved her in ways she'd never even known existed.

"The fact that I was your first makes me love you all the more," he said. Sarah had previously believed having sex outside of marriage was wrong, but now she was so in love with Ace, and she knew one day they would be married. She felt that somehow this justified their relationship.

During the month they'd been together, Ace had bought her new clothes, perfume, music, and DVDs. He told her that he had never met anyone like her, that she was special and their love was eternal. They talked about living a wonderful life together. No one had ever cared for her in the way Ace did, and she was convinced he was right about everything. She realized now that her parents didn't really love her at all. Their so-called love was just about controlling her life. His love showed her what she really wanted, not just what *they* wanted her to be.

Admittedly, he did sometimes hurt her. Nonetheless, she wanted to be with him all the time. She would do anything for Ace. She had recently come to believe that's what a person does when it's true love.

She knew there were other girls in Ace's life, but he told her that she was the only one he really cared about. "That's the biz," he said. He was referring to the "dating service" where Maggie "worked." He told her he had to mingle with all the girls to keep them on the straight and narrow.

20

She guessed they were prostitutes, but after meeting them, that didn't seem to matter. They were just real people. Somehow they didn't seem as bad as she'd been led to believe. And as Ace said, business was business.

Over the next few weeks, her feelings for Ace deepened. He always did little things to prove his love for her, like the time he sent all the other girls away so they could share the night together in a nice hotel. She came close to getting caught by her parents, who thought she was at her friend Sally's house. The narrow escape made her realize that if she and Ace were ever going to have the life they dreamed of, she would have to leave home. She was prepared to do whatever it took to preserve their love.

Fake Love and Real Love

One day Sarah drove over to Ace's for their usual lunchtime together. "I have to move to Vegas, and I want you to come with me," he told her. "I can't live without you, Sarah. I've never loved anyone the way I love you, and we will be so happy there. No more hassles from your parents, and we can be together all the time."

They left for Vegas about an hour later, after ditching Sarah's car in the school parking lot. When they reached Sacramento twelve hours later, they met up with some of Ace's friends.

"We need money, baby. All the other girls are back in Seattle. I know you'll be with me in your heart, but I need you to do these guys for us."

Sarah was surprised, but she knew the game. Besides, no matter what, she and Ace were together. She would think of him while she was with the others.

The next morning, Sarah was still reliving the nightmare of the night before. She had heard of gang rape, but she had never been roughed up and humiliated as she had that night. Part of Sarah wanted to believe that she and Ace would soon have their life together in the big, beautiful house they had talked about.

As she handed Ace the cash from the night before, Ace questioned her firmly to be sure she was giving him all of the money, including tips. He tried to tone down his demands by saying, "That's the biz; you know that." And she did know that. Pimps always get 100 percent of the earnings. "Don't worry, baby, we're going to be living the dream soon," Ace said. But despite his assurances that she wouldn't have to do this forever, Sarah knew she had just been turned out and was now a "working girl." She had no doubts about her new nightly duties. Men would pay her for sex, and she would bring the money back to Ace. A mere three months after she'd met Maggie, a life of pain and pretending had just begun.

□ □ □

Sarah's parents never quit looking for her. They searched up and down the West Coast, as well as in Reno, Vegas, and Phoenix. Although they hadn't found any trace of their daughter, Sarah's mother still knew in her heart that Sarah was alive. One day the phone rang.

"Sarah's been found," the detective on the case announced. "She's in Las Vegas."

Though "the life" had been extremely hard on Sarah, she had been afraid to leave, and there was a strange and unexplainable desire in her heart to stay. Despite all that, she found herself relieved that the raid on the brothel where Ace had placed her had rescued her from the life. Many times over the year she had feared she would be killed. Yet, she wasn't willing to talk with her parents. She was embarrassed, knowing full well what an enormous disappointment she'd proven to be. Law enforcement had to call her parents anyway.

When her parents walked into the room at the juvenile hall where the now seventeen-year-old Sarah sat in a brown overstuffed chair with her head hanging down, she didn't look up. Sarah's formerly fit body was skinny, and her skin was pale and sickly looking. Her pretty, naturally curly blonde hair barely covered the tattoo on the back of her neck where Ace had branded her as his property. Her mother knelt by the chair where Sarah sat with her hands covering her face in shame.

"Sare-Bear, I love you," her mom blubbered between her tears. "You are the most beautiful sight I have ever seen."

As they fell into each other's arms in sobs, her dad's long arms encompassed them both, and the three of them cried together. There would be many decisions to make, many tough days ahead, but Sarah was reunited with her parents, who had never stopped loving her.

A National Crisis

Sarah's story has a happier ending than most. She was able to get into a Los Angeles shelter called Children of the Night, where young girls who have been rescued out of sex trafficking are provided with the services they need to recover from their traumatic experiences. She received, among other things, treatment for the venereal diseases she had contracted, counseling for her emotional scars, and a diploma when she completed her high school education.

Unlike Sarah, however, too many human trafficking victims never escape their horrific lives, partly due to the fact that many of us have no idea this is even a problem in our communities. It may come as a surprise to learn that the National Center for Missing and Exploited Children estimates that well over one hundred thousand children are trafficked yearly in America.[1] While many of these young victims are runaways or foster children, others are from what would be considered "good" families and have been lured or coerced into human trafficking by clever predators. "These predators are particularly adept at reading children and knowing what their vulnerabilities are," says FBI Deputy Assistant Director Chip Burrus, founder of Innocence Lost, a project addressing child and teen sex trafficking.[2]

But human trafficking in this country doesn't just take place where sex is sold. Labor trafficking, which occurs on the streets, in homes, in factories, in fields, and any number of other places, is also big business.

Authorities estimate that

- there are 27 million slaves in the world today, more slaves than during the transatlantic slave trade;[3]
- human trafficking is tied with arms dealing as the second largest criminal enterprise and is the fastest growing;[4]
- about 80 percent of all trafficked individuals are female; about 50 percent are children;[5]
- 70 percent of those female victims are trafficked for sexual exploitation;[6] and
- between 244,000 and 325,000 American youth are considered at risk for sexual exploitation, and an estimated 199,000 incidents of sexual exploitation of minors occur each year in the United States.[7]

The above figures, however, are limited estimates of youth at risk for human trafficking and do not take into consideration adult US citizens trafficked for sex or American children and adults trafficked for labor.[8] Each year, an estimated $150 billion is generated by victims of human trafficking, $99 billion of which comes from sex trafficking and $51 billion from other forms of trafficking.[9] A few more disturbing statistics:

- Each year, between 14,500 and 17,500 people are trafficked into the United States from other countries.[10]
- One study estimates 30 percent of shelter youth and 70 percent of street youth are victims of commercial sexual exploitation. They may be coerced into prostitution for "survival sex" to meet daily needs for food, shelter, or drugs.[11]
- Nationally, 450,000 children run away from home each year. One out of every three teens on the street will be lured toward sex trafficking within forty-eight hours of leaving home. Statistically, this means at least 150,000 children lured into sex trafficking each year.[12]
- Average age of entry into sex trafficking is 12–14 for girls and 11–13 for boys.[13]
- One study out of Portland, Oregon, found that 96.4 percent of the victims in the study were female, close to 2.8 percent were males, and 0.9 percent were transgender.[14] (Please note: these numbers are from the Portland study and may not be representative of all populations.)
- The same study found that 49.1 percent of the youth who were served by social services had a gang connection.[15]

Admittedly, these numbers are guesstimates based on the best data available today. The hidden nature of the crime makes exact numbers difficult to come by. We all want to see human trafficking statistics because they help us get our minds around the problem. However, with these types of crimes, even those statistics obtained by expert researchers conducting studies with the greatest degree of accuracy possible under the circumstances become best guesses. You can well imagine victims of human trafficking are not able or willing to raise their hands to be counted. Still, these studies help us understand that human trafficking is a problem of epidemic proportions.

How is it possible that all of this takes place right here in the United States, and yet we don't hear much about it? Somehow we have operated under the misconception that this crime only happens overseas in places like Bangkok, Thailand, where many of us have heard about children being trafficked for sex; in the villages of India, where slaves do backbreaking work crushing rock for sixteen to eighteen hours a day; and in Russian cities, where young women are recruited and shipped to other countries. Unfortunately, though, it happens right here in our country.

Why Focus on the United States?

Many people don't think about the sale of human beings happening right here in America. If we consider the possibility of human trafficking within our borders, our assumption may be that it's confined to Las Vegas, New York, Los Angeles, and other large cities. Even those who recognize that human trafficking is as much an American disgrace as an international one sometimes don't realize this crime doesn't just occur in our big cities. Although human trafficking has certainly been discovered in large urban areas, it can flourish in upper-class suburbs, rural areas, and even in small towns like the one in which I live.

Human trafficking happens in upper-middle-class neighborhoods where people who travel or do business internationally "invest" in domestic help, who upon arrival in America can become modern slaves.

In search of a cost-effective workforce, resort communities, hotels, and country clubs sometimes unknowingly hire agencies that are actually fronts for slave labor.

In places where regular conferences are held—including but not limited to political and business conferences—as well as at large sporting events, sex-trafficked individuals are made available because traffickers know there are consumers with money who will buy them.

Finally, as you'll read in chapter 3, even church elders have unwittingly supported human traffickers.

That's why whenever I am presented with a reasonable (and sometimes, I must confess, not completely reasonable) opportunity to enlighten folks about the modern slavery that's happening all around us, I take it, because I know the extent to which this problem permeates our land. Its prominence here makes sense if you think about it. Human trafficking follows money. America, being the richest nation in the world, stands to reward human traffickers with some of the highest profits anywhere.

In February 2014, my husband and I visited the 9/11 Tribute Center, where guides share their personal stories of surviving the September 11, 2001, terror attacks. We walked around and heard story after story of the horrific killings or, as 9/11 survivors prefer to call it, *mass murder* that occurred on that day. Our minds were reeling with grief for our country and those who had lost lives or loved ones and all whose lives had been forever scarred by this horrific crime.

True stories circulated of murder, torture, devastation, and complete disregard for precious human lives that were left in the rubble that day, but Americans didn't give the terrorists the expected response of living in fear. Instead, we banded together, bringing help for survivors and for the families of those who had been horrifically murdered in the attack. We linked arms and began rebuilding. All across the country, American flags waved proudly from storefronts, from atop high buildings, in car windows, and in the back of pickup trucks driving down the road.

I remember the constant coverage on television, on the radio, and in the print media. We articulated our grief at cash registers and dinner tables, in classrooms and in our prayers. We aired our pain about this horrific tragedy and pledged to never forget. We brainstormed about what each of us could do to ensure it never happens again.

Our visit to the Twin Towers site took place just after I had spent some weeks preparing for and working in intense anti–human trafficking efforts surrounding the Super Bowl held in East Rutherford, New Jersey. I couldn't help but make a comparison: Our nation is experiencing another national tragedy. This crime of human trafficking is affecting untold thousands of people through murder, torture, rape, and complete dehumanization.

It is time for our country to link arms, as we did after 9/11, against this crime that not only has occurred but continues to occur, not just in a few places but all across our nation. None of us is immune to human trafficking touching our lives or the lives of those we love. We must work to fight it and keep talking about it; we must take a visible stand against human trafficking. We must provide services for those whose lives have been horrifically affected by this crime committed against them. We must band together to treat them as heroes who have been victimized and honor them for having the courage to endure and finally get help, not treat them as a dirty part of our society we are afraid to touch.

What if instead of condemning them for their "bad choices"—since most never had a choice at all—we as a society embraced them and provided them with driver's licenses and other basic identification that has been stripped from them? What if we offered them shelter and counseling, even if the pain of their trauma causes them to run time and time again? What if we helped them until they can help themselves, which may take many, many years? What if we worked for better laws to provide services for the victims/survivors and stiff penalties for the traffickers?

All the traffickers ask is that we do nothing. We must never provide them that luxury. We must never forget.

Thankfully, many anti-trafficking groups have sprung up in the United States in the past few years. We are not in a third world country where one can often go to the corner and enlist a police officer's assistance in finding a brothel or in buying a child for sex. For the most part, our law enforcement officials work hard to uphold the law. If we can do the following things, we can eradicate human trafficking in the United States in our lifetime:

- Raise awareness to the point of the general public knowing what human trafficking looks like and what to do if they see it.
- Adequately educate law enforcement officials and the courts.
- Enact laws that uphold justice against traffickers and sex buyers.
- Provide adequate services for victims and survivors.

I believe if we link arms and do all we can, we can eradicate this atrocity in the United States and around the globe. It is wrong for anyone to be enslaved, no matter where it occurs.

Modern Slavery

So what exactly is human trafficking? Why is it sometimes called slavery?

Human trafficking is the recruitment, harboring, transporting, obtaining, or maintaining of a person by means of force, fraud, or coercion for purposes of involuntary servitude, debt bondage, slavery, or a commercial sex act or any commercial sex act in which the person performing the act is under eighteen years old.[16] And while the word *trafficking* denotes movement, physical movement is not a requisite. As my friend Lauran Bethell says, trafficking is the exploitation of vulnerability. Trafficking by its very nature implies movement—and the movement is from vulnerability to the exploitation of that vulnerability.[17]

Human trafficking, in my estimation, is one of the worst atrocities happening in the world at this time. It is deliberate control, manipulation, force, and torture of a human being whose rights have been overtaken by another human being. In fact, it has been officially labeled a form of torture by Halleh Seddighzadeh, a forensic traumatologist and doctoral resident specializing in the psychological treatment of extreme forms of traumatic stress.[18]

An old adage says, "An ounce of prevention is worth a pound of cure." One study conducted in Minnesota found that to be true regarding human trafficking. The study showed that for early intervention for female youth, "there was a return on investment of $34 in benefit for each $1 in cost." The idea that prevention is a huge and valuable part of this work has been confirmed by this study.[19]

Earlier in this chapter you read about Sarah, a young girl from a nice home being lured into forced prostitution. As sketchy as the statistics are, we know that roughly 800,000 children are reported missing in the United States a year; that equates to roughly 2,200 every day.[20] A good percentage of those kids wind up as human trafficking victims.

Marc Klaas of KlaasKids, an organization he established in 1994 to give meaning to the kidnap and murder of his then twelve-year-old daughter, Polly Hannah Klaas, told me during my interview with him that the issue of human trafficking is possibly one of the most important issues of our day.[21] Having created a legacy in her name that will be protective of children for generations to come, he now works tirelessly to raise awareness and help find missing children, some of whom may have been trafficked.

Some—perhaps most—of the children in America who become victims of human trafficking are forced into sex trafficking. In fact, according to Ernie Allen, former president and CEO of the National Center for Missing and Exploited Children, who spoke before the US House of Representatives, "Researchers also estimated that one-third of street-level prostitutes in the United States are less than eighteen, while half of off-street prostitutes are less than eighteen. With the explosion in the sale of kids for sex online, it is clear that more kids are at risk today than ever before."[22] As noted earlier in this chapter, as many as one in three teen runaways will be lured into sex slavery within forty-eight hours of leaving home, and the emotional impact on these youngsters is devastating. One study found that 71 percent of trafficked children exhibit suicidal tendencies.[23]

And children represent just one segment of those being trafficked in our country. Individuals are imprisoned (whether bodily or emotionally), often abused physically and sexually, and forced to perform for hours on end for little to no money. If that sounds like slavery to you, you are entirely correct. Indeed, the term *human trafficking*, which we used to describe Sarah's situation, is simply a politically correct phrase for what is really modern slavery.

How Can This Happen?

Unfortunately, it's quite simple. There are people motivated by greed and profit who are willing to use others for their financial gain, regardless of the pain and suffering they impose. The fact that few of us suspect—or even believe—that it is happening here gives the traffickers an unparalleled leg up. I have often said that the only thing traffickers ask of us is that we remain silent about this atrocity and do nothing.

Added to that, when trafficking *is* exposed, the proof required to bring the perpetrators to justice makes prosecution very difficult.

We have much work to do within our legal system so that traffickers may be brought to justice.

In our country's earlier history, slavery was legal—and even socially acceptable. However, in the 1850s, a slave didn't come without a cost. Purchasing a slave to work the fields or in the house, no matter how odious that now seems, was quite an investment, with a cost equivalent to about $40,000 in today's economy.[24]

Now, 165 years later, the cost of a slave has diminished greatly. Some say the average price is about $100. When I interviewed one ex-pimp, he finished my sentence for me when I began, "The cost of a slave today is . . . ?"

"Nothing," he asserted.[25] He knew from experience how little he'd paid to acquire sex slaves to work for him.

If we think of an item that costs $40,000, most of us would first envision a vehicle. In doing some research, I found that you can purchase a brand-new Mercedes-Benz C-Class for under $40,000. If you bought a shiny new red Mercedes for $40,000, you would probably be careful how you drove it. You would wash it, maybe even by hand, and regularly give it the tune-ups it needs along with all the recommended maintenance. In short, you would look after it carefully to ensure that your investment was being maintained.

On the other hand, if you could get that same Mercedes for $100 or less, and you knew you could buy as many as you wanted at that price, you would probably simply trade it in for a new model or dispose of it instead of bothering to do the simplest of things like tune-ups or buying new tires. That's exactly what today's modern slaveholders do.

Today's slaveholder reasons that it doesn't make sense to invest in the maintenance of a slave who can be replaced for a very small amount of money. If a slave will cost the slaveholder a significant amount of time, money, or hassle, the slave is discarded like a broken DVD player not worth repairing.

This principle is graphically portrayed in the 2005 Lifetime miniseries *Human Trafficking*. In one scene, a child sex slave in Manila has developed a high fever. Concerned about the life and health of her friend, another child sex slave in the same seedy brothel attempts to secure medical help for her pal by telling the trafficker about the girl's condition. The next scene shows the trafficker coming in, picking up the sick preteen, taking her outside the brothel, breaking her innocent neck, and disposing of her body as the first girl helplessly witnesses her friend's murder.

Slaveholders in the United States may or may not murder their slaves; however, they certainly do not invest in their well-being. Food can be scarce, often just enough to keep the slave alive. Medical care is almost nonexistent. And as with the slavery in our country's past, regard for human life isn't even part of the equation.

One of the most popular card games in the Wild West was faro, in which gamblers wagered money, livestock, and slaves. It was a common occurrence for a slave master to return home, pull a slave out of their quarters, and send them to work for the game's winner.

That hasn't changed. "Girls can get traded from a card game or dice roll," says an ex-pimp I interviewed. "You could lose a girl and a girl would have to go. I mean, if you're in a pimp situation with a prostitute, you should [be able to] say right now, 'Guess what you get to do, you get to go be with him' and I'm not talking about dating. 'You can be with him now for good.' You should have that much control in theory because of how you set up your life."[26]

Using people as replaceable commodities is what human trafficking—or modern slavery—is all about. So it's not surprising to find pimps advertising people like products in big cities and even in small-town USA. In the age of the internet, online listings make this even easier.

An example of one such online ad during the 2014 Super Bowl in New Jersey showed several pictures of a scantily clad young teen.

Please note, though the ad sounds like this teen is excited to solicit such an encounter, the pimp or trafficker directs all these ads and requires such "pretty please" attitudes to be portrayed. The ad read:

> Hi, you hott, sexy and freaky guys out there looking for fun!
>
> I'm also looking forwards to having some exotic fun. I'm that nice shape petite little lady that you have been wanting to take advantage of all of your life. So if you are one of these guys with you can reach me at ***-***-****.
>
> No private calls or text messages will be answered. Now you are just buttons away. See you soon.

It is difficult to understand the depth of depravity that is required to sell or buy human beings in this manner. Make no mistake, the purpose behind all of this is money. But please don't confuse it with a legitimate business. This is about the sale of human flesh.

Some ads are much more graphic, with nude photos and detailed descriptions of sexual acts that leave nothing to one's imagination as the perpetrators try to squeeze the most money out of every pound of human flesh sold. The methods are always changing as these criminals try to stay one step ahead of law enforcement.

Craigslist, which was one of the first online sites to offer these thinly veiled "sex for sale" ads, voluntarily removed its adult services section after pressure by seventeen state attorneys general. In competition for the dollars of those who are buying human flesh, other sites have been developed since the Craigslist adult services closure.

In a 2011–12 effort led by then president of the National Association of Attorneys General, Washington State Attorney General Rob McKenna pressured another online site, Backpage, to remove sex ads. Backpage has repeatedly refused to discontinue the ads, from which they make a purported $22 million per year off of those who are, more often than not, sex-trafficked individuals. McKenna said, "It will take a cultural shift to change attitudes about prostitution.

People look at prostitution and think it's a choice, but there are very few, if any, volunteers. The more we learn about sex trafficking, the more we believe it is dominated by individuals exploiting both children and adults."[27]

One can only hope that the people who control those websites will wake up to the reality that they are, in fact, accessories to the crime. I would ask them—and you—to compare the online ad above with this slave auction flyer from 1829:

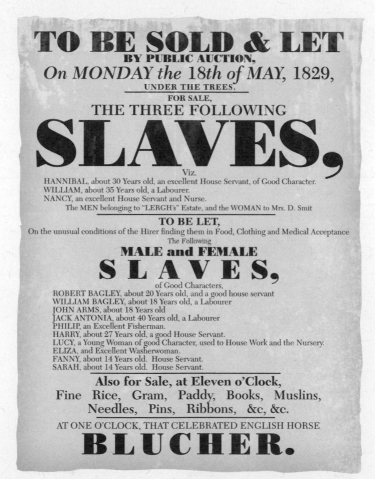

TO BE SOLD & LET
BY PUBLIC AUCTION,
On MONDAY the 18th of MAY, 1829,
UNDER THE TREES.
FOR SALE,
THE THREE FOLLOWING
SLAVES,
Viz.
HANNIBAL, about 30 Years old, an excellent House Servant, of Good Character.
WILLIAM, about 35 Years old, a Labourer.
NANCY, an excellent House Servant and Nurse.
The MEN belonging to "LERGH's" Estate, and the WOMAN to Mrs. D. Smit

TO BE LET,
On the unusual conditions of the Hirer finding them in Food, Clothing and Medical Acceptance
The Following
MALE and FEMALE
SLAVES,
of Good Characters,
ROBERT BAGLEY, about 20 Years old, and a good house servant
WILLIAM BAGLEY, about 18 Years old, a Labourer
JOHN ARMS, about 18 Years old
JACK ANTONIA, about 40 Years old, a Labourer
PHILIP, an Excellent Fisherman.
HARRY, about 27 Years old, a good House Servant.
LUCY, a Young Woman of good Character, used to House Work and the Nursery.
ELIZA, and Excellent Washerwoman.
FANNY, about 14 Years old. House Servant.
SARAH, about 14 Years old. House Servant.

Also for Sale, at Eleven o'Clock,
Fine Rice, Gram, Paddy, Books, Muslins,
Needles, Pins, Ribbons, &c, &c.
AT ONE O'CLOCK, THAT CELEBRATED ENGLISH HORSE
BLUCHER.

You'll note that in addition to the sale of slaves, commodities are also advertised on the poster. Similarly, one can shop for furniture, clothing, food, jobs, and other items on many websites selling sex.

Trafficking Victims Protection Act (TVPA)

Fortunately, trafficking victims, survivors, and those of us trying to help them now have some laws that can help bring justice to perpetrators and provide some services for victims. The judicial process has begun, but there is still a tremendous need for better laws and more services.

In the mid-1990s the US government began to recognize the need for laws to specifically address the crime of human trafficking. Congressman Chris Smith of New Jersey has been a champion against human trafficking and authored the original Trafficking Victims Protection Act (TVPA), which was signed into law by President Bill Clinton in 2000. It has since been updated and will continue to be updated to provide better protection from, prevention of, and prosecution of the crime of human trafficking. Victims and survivors now have legal rights as well as access to services. Those perpetuating these crimes within our borders and American citizens who travel outside the United States for sex tourism can be criminally prosecuted.

Stopping Demand

Ultimately, however, one of the main keys to stopping human trafficking extends beyond the legal system to all of us. In the universal law of supply and demand, if there were no demand, there would be no need for supply. Consumers insisting on manufactured or agricultural product lines that can be proven to be free of slave labor, for example, can reduce labor trafficking and help eliminate the sale of slave-produced products.

Sex trafficking is particularly dependent on demand. Without consumers viewing pornography online, without sex buyers willing to pay for sex, there would be no need for sex-trafficked individuals. Just like one can shop online for clothing, online sex ads allow the sex buyer many choices. When buying a human for sex, they can choose based on age, the color of skin or hair, or particular fetishes. They will have more choices than if one were going online to buy a shirt from a large online mall. As long as people are sold like a commodity for sexual services and buyers continue to frequent those ads, the demand for human beings will continue.

Helping to Stop Human Trafficking

The question is: *What are we going to do about this unconscionable situation?*

We will probably each have a different answer to that question because we are each different individuals with different talents and gifts. As for myself, I am working to increase awareness and partnering with legislators, law enforcement, and other organizations to fight this atrocity among us.

I would also like to challenge you to ask, "What am *I* supposed to do to help fight this abomination?" I can't answer that question for you, but I have listed below the first of many suggestions you will find in this book. Some will take short amounts of time, while others will require more effort. All will help the fight against human trafficking.

For example, volunteering even limited time with nonprofit organizations effectively fighting the crime of human trafficking does

37

more to help than you could possibly imagine. At our local chapter of Oregonians Against Trafficking Humans (OATH), we couldn't do nearly as much without the help of two of our volunteers.

Kristina is a quiet, busy young woman who, with her husband, owns and operates a successful and rapidly growing karate school. They allow us to use that space for occasional meetings. Kristina helps me whenever I'm challenged with clerical duties (which is often). She also makes phone calls, oversees other volunteers, edits copy, and even designs knockout posters and flyers. In the few hours a week she puts in, Kristina has even connected us with an accountant who has donated services to our organization. She has a knack of looking for and tending to things that need to be done. In and of themselves, her deeds may seem small, but they add up to a huge contribution to our organization.

Another volunteer is Christi, a single mom who works hard to support her children and who would be busy with even half the things she does. She serves one of our organization's most vital functions by regularly sending reminders and supporting our "viral" efforts to get the word out about events via email, Facebook, and other social media. When we had a large event, Christi distributed the majority of hundreds of our posters. I teased her that she's never met a blank space on a wall that she didn't think deserved a poster.

Christi and Kristina are strong soldiers in this fight against human trafficking. Countless numbers of people and leads come to us as a result of their efforts to spread the word about stopping human trafficking in our area. They're a vital part of our work. Their selfless efforts have helped to rescue victims and save lives. While these two women are local heroes to me, even small, one-time acts such as making phone calls, allowing a poster to be hung in your business, or writing a letter to Congress can help make a significant difference.

Although not everyone can or wants to donate time, monetary contributions can be just as important. Antislavery awareness organizations and groups that aid in the recovery and rehabilitation of newly freed slaves share a common and desperate need for funding. Educating the public about human trafficking, freeing individual slaves, and providing care and rehabilitation for survivors isn't cheap. The only way these organizations can continue their work is through generous donations from concerned people. Even small, regular donations of $10 a month help give antislavery organizations financial stability and can be more effective than paying hundreds or even thousands of dollars to participate in a short-term effort overseas. When you cheerfully give either time or money to antislavery organizations, you become a partner in the fight against human trafficking.

We often hear objectionable activities protested with the chant "Not in my backyard." There is even an acronym—NIMBY—for that saying. However, the truth is that human trafficking *is already happening* in your backyard and mine. Until we acknowledge not only that modern slavery happens but that it's occurring under our noses, and until we are willing to speak up when we see something that looks like it might be human trafficking, this atrocity will continue.

For Discussion

1. How would you define human trafficking or modern slavery?

2. If Sarah had been informed about human trafficking and how a trafficker grooms a potential victim, do you think she would have fallen prey to Maggie and Ace? Why or why not?

3. What could you personally do to help your community become aware that modern slavery exists?

4. Find a recent news item that concerns human trafficking and discuss it.

   - How could it have been prevented?

   - How can you help prevent a similar situation from occurring in your community?

   - Who can you have a conversation with to make a difference?

2

Eyes That See, Hearts That Care, Hands That Help

I want you to be concerned about your next door neighbor.
Do you know your next door neighbor?

—Mother Teresa

Given Kachepa,[1] now a young man in his twenties, stood at his father's Zambia gravesite, to which he, his siblings, and other family members had hiked through snake-infested, six-foot-high weeds and underbrush. The pain of missing his parents returned. Still, visiting their resting places had brought him peace. He had come home.

There was a time Given had thought this would never happen. He thought he would never escape the Baptist missionary, Keith Grimes, who had taken him and other boys from his poor African

41

community to the United States to sing in a choir and supposedly live a better life. And without Sandy Shepherd—an American wife, mother, and devoted Christian—and others like her, he might still be enduring the brutal mistreatment to which he'd been subjected for so long.

It was 1999. Eleven-year-old Given leaned against the wall, his arms wrapped around his knees. He was in the back bedroom of the double-wide mobile home where he lived for months with anywhere from twelve to twenty-two other boys. Some, like Given, were members of the Zambian Acapella Boys Choir II; members of other choirs were also working for the Teachers Teaching Teachers (TTT) ministry. Despite his exhaustion, along with the fear and hopelessness that come from being crammed into such a small space, Given concentrated on trying to remain positive. But even with air-conditioning, the Texas sun made the inside of the trailer home feel hot and humid and seemed to intensify his misery.

Being tired and weak, he didn't feel he had the energy to shovel the stone-hard Texas soil one more time today. He and the rest of the boys from the choir had been so delighted when a few months earlier Pastor Keith had said, "You want a swimming pool? Wouldn't it be fun to have a swimming pool?" Little did they realize they would be forced to dig it themselves with shovels and picks. Today, as usual, they had been awakened at 7:00 a.m. and made to go out and run, then ate breakfast and worked on excavating the future pool. Hours later, despite bone-crushing fatigue, they had begun choir rehearsal. Given knew that they wouldn't get anything more to eat until they'd finished their five hours of practice. As growing teen and preteen boys, they were naturally hungry, which increased their suffering for lack of food.

The meal would be meager at best, consisting mainly of a dish called *nshima*, which was similar to cornmeal mush. He knew better than to complain. Punishment for complaints about the lack of food or their extreme fatigue, or for inquiries about why they weren't getting the schooling they had been promised, ranged from verbal assaults to having the gas to the double-wide trailer turned off, making it impossible for them to even cook their *nshima*.

This was not the picture that Pastor Keith had painted of the lives Given and the others would live in America when Given had auditioned for the choir in his hometown of Kalingalinga, Zambia. Pastor Keith had promised the comfort of shelter, plenty of food, and a good education. Life in Zambia was so difficult. It had been easy for Pastor Keith to convince the locals that any life in America would be an improvement. Given couldn't wait. He was most excited about the opportunity to earn money so he could help his family. Even though he wasn't the oldest, somehow he had always felt responsible for the care of all his siblings, especially his younger sister, Doreen, and his oldest sister, Grace. Now Grace was suffering from tuberculosis, the same disease that had taken his mom. He couldn't bear the thought of also losing her to that horrific disease. He had to find a way to buy the medical attention she needed.

Given had been just seven when his mom died. Though he hardly remembered her, he still recalled the comforting smell of her body when she used to hold him close. He was too young to attend her funeral, but he often thought of her and tried to hold remnants of her in his heart and mind.

When Given was nine, his father died. "My world fell apart," he says. "I helped build my father's coffin and remember looking at him, thinking he could speak." Given recalled going with his uncles and aunts to his father's funeral and seeing the metal and glass plate his uncle placed as a marker at the head of his father's grave. They did that so they would know where his father was buried when they wanted to return. Given had dreamed for years of going back to the grave and visiting his father, but it was two hours through the bush from their town. He hoped his dad was proud of him, even though he hadn't been able to bring in as much money for the family as he had hoped.

As a child—and an orphan—Given looked constantly for any kind of available work. He broke stones and carried heavy loads to earn tiny amounts of cash. He carried purchases for ladies as they exited the minibus. He sold paraffin for the cooking grills. He was able to buy food and shoes for his sisters, but there was never enough left for the large sum it would cost to get medical care for Grace. He took comfort in the services he attended at Highland Baptist Church. It was there that he became a Christian and grew into the relationship with God that sustained him through the hard times. He said that prayer sustained him with the strength that he needed to get through his incredibly difficult life.

The Scam of TTT

Keith Grimes and TTT seemed like the answer to his prayers. When Given met them in 1998, the seemingly gentle and trustworthy managers talked about other boys' choirs they had brought from Zambia to the United States. They said that with the money earned putting on concerts at churches and schools, TTT would be able to fund the building of schools in Zambia. They promised that the boys who traveled to America with them would get a good school education, as well as a fair salary for performing, so they would be able to send home money to the families left behind.

This was the part that made Given the happiest. In addition to providing for his siblings while he was away, upon his return he could buy some land in Zambia and build a house where they could all live together. His big heart wanted more than anything to make life better for his family, and this chance to go to America with TTT might be his only opportunity.

The village was buzzing with talk of the lucky ones who would get to travel to America with TTT. Given practiced singing constantly, even though he knew the odds were not in his favor since he was younger and less experienced than most of the auditioning boys. Still, he was determined to try his best. When he was told he was among the chosen ones, "It was like a dream come true," says Given. "They told us they were going to give us free everything— free clothes and money." What could be better than getting paid for singing about his faith every day and getting a great education too? He hoped the paperwork would come through fast so he could go right away. His family needed money.

Although TTT had recruited and returned other choir members from Kalingalinga, Grimes's finely crafted web of deception, along with a clever campaign that discredited those who had come back, prevented Given from knowing the grim reality he would face when he came to America with them.

Sadly, his beloved sister Grace died before he could get to the United States and start sending money home. He mourned her death, and silently he prayed that no harm would come to any of his other siblings. He went to live with his aunt Margret, but with six children of her own, there was not enough food, clothing, or even blankets to keep them all fed, dry, and warm. "Some days we were lucky to get one meal."[2] Given helped her as much as he could and earned money as best he could, but at times it seemed as if the cold and poverty were dark clouds closing in on them. Still, Given felt the opportunity with TTT would be a way to help them all. News of his paperwork coming through couldn't arrive fast enough.

Finally, it was time to go to America. The flight was comfortable with plenty to eat. A tray of food all to himself? Little did he know he wouldn't experience that sense of comfort again for a long time.

When they got to America, the boys sang in churches and schools, sometimes performing as many as eight concerts a day. Pastor Keith, who had seemed so gentle and kind in Zambia, was now cruel and demanding. Schooling was nonexistent, and Given soon experienced a new kind of pain and exhaustion. When the boys pleaded for more rest and sustenance, Keith verbally abused them for challenging his authority in their lives. They were also not allowed to question why they weren't being paid as promised. Instead, Pastor Keith gave them a list of Scriptures, reminding them that they were there to be servants and were expected to obey their master. The hierarchy was both clear and coercive. Pastor Keith was in charge, and they were to be subservient. Complaints about their treatment were met with threats to return the dissenters to Zambia. The threats were real.

"I thought we were going to go to school," a few of the boys said to Pastor Keith eleven months into the tour. "When are you going to pay us for our work?" They were kicked out of the choir and turned over to the authorities for deportation. The message sent back to Kalingalinga with them would be that they had been disobedient, disrespectful, and irresponsible. Sometimes when a boy was sent back to Zambia in disgrace, his family rejected him. The Zambian community was also more prone to believe a white pastor than an "ungrateful and lazy" Zambian teenager.

While on tour, the boys stayed with host families. Although the host families often offered them gifts, the boys had been forbidden to accept them. When the host families insisted they take phone cards, sneakers, Bibles, or other gifts—or slipped gifts into their suitcases—the "contraband" would be confiscated during one of TTT's regular searches of the boys' personal belongings. Much later, it was discovered that Barbara Grimes Martens, Keith's daughter, had buried some of the gifts in the hole the boys had been forced to dig for a swimming pool. The rest of the gifts the boys had treasured had been tossed in a Dumpster.

In between concert tours, the boys were brought back to the crowded trailer in Whitesboro, Texas—that is, the middle of no-where. They were the only black individuals for many miles. Any hope of asking for help was dashed with the knowledge that people would believe the white American preacher over skinny black boys from Africa. That was one of the many things that kept the Zam-bian Boys Choir captive. "It seemed like we were free, but really we were not free, because psychologically we'd been coerced to behave in a certain way, and if we were not, they'd say, 'We are going to send you back to Zambia.'"[3]

□ □ □

Though the boys regularly saw large sums given on their behalf in the church offerings that TTT collected at their concerts, the money never reached them and did nothing to improve their living condi-tions or their treatment. They lived in a state of agitation, anger, and exhaustion, whether performing or not. When young Given collapsed during one tour, Pastor Keith told him to stand and get ready to sing. "I'm too tired and weak," Given explained. "I am exhausted."

The pastor grabbed him by the shirt, stood him up, and raged in his face. "I said get up and sing, boy. Unless you want to go home, you will sing!"

Motivated by fear and the lingering hope of a better life for him-self and his family, Given conjured up the energy to sing through the day's remaining concerts. He realized that despite the current hardships, he had no other options.

TTT's leadership had told Given that if the authorities ques-tioned him, he was to say that the boys were happy, well fed, and fairly paid and that they wanted to be there. If he didn't tell them that, they promised to send him back to Zambia in disgrace. He would never be able to help his brothers and sisters that way. He had to be strong.

Things didn't improve even after Pastor Keith died of a brain tumor in April 1999. His daughter Barbara and son-in-law Gary Martens, to whom he had turned over the operation, were just as demanding and controlling as he had been.

Good Samaritans Take Action

The law was starting to catch up with TTT. The boys had been told not to talk about TTT with host families, and TTT's leadership had told host families not to provide the choir members with any personal information that could lead to future communication. However, suspecting that the boys were being exploited, host families from previous choirs had tried to get help for their temporary charges. Phone calls and letters had been generated to federal, state, and local authorities, and the FBI was contacted along with the senators and governor of Texas. The FBI determined nothing was wrong because they did not see any handcuffs or bruises on the boys. According to Sandy, one choir member even contacted *The Oprah Winfrey Show* to see if the superstar might draw attention to this case of modern slavery. None of these calls produced help for the Zambian boys. It seemed as if no one was willing to help. But the groundwork had been laid.

In the spring of 1999, Barbara Grimes Martens demanded the Feds take away the four boys who had protested their treatment, saying they were a "physical threat." Although they were removed in handcuffs, law enforcement's investigation quickly revealed that the boys were not at fault. The Labor Department was informed, and TTT was told to begin paying the choir members. A lawsuit was filed on behalf of the choir members, prompting TTT to begin paying them, at least on the books. Behind the scenes, however, the Martenses told the boys they owed back pay for housing, food, clothing, electricity, and other expenses. Even though the Labor Department believed the boys were being paid in full, they were given only a small amount of money, about $20 per month, which was insufficient to buy the meals they were expected to purchase for themselves as they traveled from city to city.

The rescued "arrested" boys managed to get word back to Given that they had not been sent back to Zambia and had instead been placed in safe housing. That gave the remaining boys hope that they could get out as well. Finally, in January 2000, the boys demanded that Barbara Grimes Martens either pay them what she owed or call the Immigration and Naturalization Services (INS) to take them away. The INS was contacted and the boys were removed from the trailer. That's when the INS called Sandy Shepherd's church, and she was contacted and asked to help.

Sandy is an active and trusted member in her local church who regularly contributed to the choir and loves getting behind worthy causes and being a part of good things happening. But she was busy with her own family's needs. Her daughter was in a major theatrical production at school, and other pressing matters had rendered her busier than ever. Nonetheless, she felt she needed to house these boys so they wouldn't have to spend the night in a holding cell. Her mother heart knew that after all they'd been through they needed a place to stay where they would feel safe.

Sandy's sense of responsibility for the boys extended past that one night. After three months, she single-handedly managed to place each of them in long-term homes. Given went to West Texas to live but returned to visit the Shepherds in August 2000. During his visit, the host mom sent Given a letter indicating that because of her health problems she could no longer house him. By that point, the Shepherds' last child had left for college, so they took in Given as their own. He has appeared in every family portrait since.

Given worked hard to improve his English. "In seventh grade I would go to class and I didn't understand a single thing that the teacher said. If I had a paper to write, sometimes it'd take me six or seven hours to get done because I wasn't understanding what was going on in class." He decided he would learn twenty new words a day, and he drilled himself on those and practiced using them in conversations.[4]

Given worked hard in school and feels that persistence is the key to achieving his goals. He tells young people now, "Life is very difficult for anybody, but you just have to keep pushing and eventually you're going to reach your goal."[5]

But he didn't just work hard at school. Through the odd jobs he's held since starting high school, Given has sent money back to help his family in Zambia on a regular basis. His earnings allowed his brother to build a four-bedroom home where his family lives.

This young man who at one time struggled with speaking English knows how to achieve goals. He graduated from the University of North Texas and is in his last year at Baylor School of Dentistry. He will be a full-fledged dentist soon, and after he has paid his school loans, his next goal remains the same as it has been since the day he left for America at age eleven: going back to Zambia to help his family and other Zambians.

One other promise has been fulfilled as well: Sandy and Deetz Shepherd and other host families opened a school for the Zambian Acapella Boys Choir in Kalingalinga, making good on Grimes's empty promise years before regarding education. That school still serves the community with high school classes.

Not all trafficking stories have an ending this happy and wonderful. This is a good example of a community linking arms and doing what they can for the good of all. Given is right when he says, "You're going to go through hardships . . . you just put your head down . . . you trust in God . . . you're going to reach your goal."[6]

A Dream Fulfilled

After what seemed like a lifetime, Given returned to Zambia with Sandy Shepherd in 2011 to reunite with his siblings, family, and friends. It had been eleven and a half years since they had seen each other. Given, now a grown man, looked very different than the eleven-year-old who boarded that giant plane in 1998.

After he'd sat for days with his siblings getting reacquainted, Given set out to find his parents' resting places. He had been so young when his mother died. Witnessing kids and mothers interacting during all those stays in host homes had made Given wonder what his life would have been like if his mother had survived.

He was grateful for Sandy and Deetz Shepherd. They had given him so much and had shown him love in ways he'd never known in Zambia or with TTT. He loved them and thought of them as his American parents. In return, they too loved him like he was their own flesh and blood. But Given knew he had to find his roots. It was a part of who he was, and he needed to know.

The day he and his aunt, Margret, found his mother's grave had a bittersweet flavor. Hand-dug graves, mound after mound covering a thousand acres, were overgrown with weeds that were especially high and thick in the rainy season. Margret remembered a mango tree being near her sister's grave. Finally, after digging through the grass on different mounds in the area near the mango tree, they spotted the small piece of metal with the correct number on it.

Given was relieved to find the spot where his mom rested. As he and Aunt Margret shared stories of his mom, he was surprised at the peace he felt. When he was a little boy, they had taken his mama's body away to a place that he couldn't visit. He had missed her terribly and dreamed of where she might be. Now he knew, and he felt the peace and the pain of closure.

Sandy Shepherd watched her son from a respectful distance. Her heart ached for him and for the mother he had lost at such a young age, and yet she was pleased that he had this moment. She knew this was hard on Given, but the experience was giving him a much-needed part of the puzzle of himself. As Given walked away from his mother's grave, he broke off the top of a large wild plant and grasped it tightly in his hand. Taking it with him back to America would be important to his healing. Somehow this weed from near his mother's grave would remind him that he hadn't been abandoned or rejected.

Later that week, he set out to find his father's grave. This time, much of his family—aunts, uncles, brothers, sisters, and cousins—joined him. Sandy also came to lend her support. The group walked for the better part of two hours, deep into the dense bush where the threat of snakes and other creatures was very real. They also walked through cornfields, through weeds taller than they were, and over terrain so steep that they had to slide down in order to get through. Finally, they found the area that Given and the others recognized as his father's burial site.

Given had now completed the trek to see his family. As he walked away from his dad's grave, he broke off the top of another weed. Joined with his first picking, these little pieces from where his parents lay would remind him that he was loved—by his mom and dad, by his families in Zambia and America, and by a God who had rescued him.

Certainly Given had been given an incredible second chance at life. In spite of feeling abandoned and abused at the hands of a cruel trafficker, in spite of narrowly escaping a life of poverty and disease in Zambia and a life of slavery in America, Given felt that God had taken good care of him by redeeming him to a beautiful family, an education, and a new life. The faith he adopted in Zambia sustained him through his enslavement and continues to sustain him. Because Given has chosen to forgive TTT members, he now lives as a survivor, no longer captive to his victimization. In listening to him talk of his experience, one doesn't hear a trace of resentment or unforgiveness for what happened to him. Instead of living a life of bitterness, he lives a life of gratitude and deep character, which has enabled him to soar to levels he could have never even dreamed of.

How Many Slaves Work for *You*?

Sometimes, despite our best intentions, we get misled. The Shepherds, for example, generously supported the Zambian boys' choir before they knew the truth about what was happening to the boys and where the money was going.

We have all unsuspectingly helped to perpetuate human trafficking. We don't mean to. Most of us have no idea we're doing it. Those of us who understand the prevalence of trafficking in our Western society abhor the idea that we are unintentionally contributing to modern slavery. But understanding that we are part of the problem can prompt us to be part of the solution. If we have the courage to look at how we have participated and to challenge ourselves, we become an immense force for eliminating the human trafficking crisis that causes so much suffering in this country and around the world.

Each of us must be willing to utilize the tools we have available to answer the question, "What is my part in this atrocity, and how much am I contributing?" An organization called Slavery Footprint is prepared to deliver that uncomfortable information to you for free at www.slaveryfootprint.org.

I was afraid to take this quiz because I had heard other abolitionists recount their high scores. Knowing how much I work to be slave-free, I hoped my score would be very low. As I took the online test, I was careful to be honest but not overestimate any of my usages . . . and I was *shocked* at the number of slaves it said I employ. I don't think the results were entirely accurate, but I am truly careful to buy local, fair-trade produce and other items. And let's face it: even one slave is far too many.

But how can we change the fact that just being a part of Western culture makes us a part of supporting slavery? Even if we are careful and have dedicated our lives to fighting this atrocity, by our very participation in society we are supporting slavery. The solution isn't to hibernate and live off the land in the woods. There are practical things we can do while living in the real world.

The first step involves simply becoming aware. Right now you can give yourself a pat on the back because you have begun reading this book, which will make you much more aware of human trafficking. As painful as it is, we need to think about Given and so many other people forced into servitude. Instead of turning away, we need to turn our heartfelt sympathy into empathy, which prompts action. We need to bear the pain of knowing and extend a hand.

Each of us can do something, whether it's talking to our neighbors about the issue of human trafficking, donating time and/or money to anti-trafficking groups, or praying to stop this atrocity. But we also need to look at how we let this happen and why we all aren't up in arms. That means challenging the hierarchy that has encouraged our blindness.

The Targets

Trafficking attacks the vulnerable—primarily women and children but also men such as Mexican farmworkers who lack social stature and money. It's easy to look down on those less fortunate than ourselves, especially when they're walking the streets in a sleazy outfit, cleaning toilets, or sewing the garments we wear. They're not like us. They're not at our level, so they're not as valuable as we are. No one ever says it that bluntly, but our actions expose our hearts.

Sad to say, even Christianity (my faith choice) has often followed the cultural interpretation of the Bible rather than its contextual intent. Many Christians were strong proponents of slavery in America during the 1800s.

> [Slavery] was established by decree of Almighty God . . . it is sanctioned in the Bible, in both Testaments, from Genesis to Revelation . . . it has existed in all ages, has been found among the people of the highest civilization, and in nations of the highest proficiency in the arts.
>
> —Jefferson Davis, president of the
> Confederate States of America[7]

> The right of holding slaves is clearly established in the Holy Scriptures, both by precept and example.
>
> —Rev. Dr. Richard Furman, president of the
> Baptist State Convention, South Carolina[8]

Scary? These days the above comments are frightening, but in the 1800s they were the accepted cultural belief and almost universally supported among Christians. If you had spoken against slavery in most churches (with the exception of among Quakers and some Wesleyans, who took strong action to rescue slaves), you might have been ousted as ignorant of the Word of God and accused of not following Christian traditions. The church was equally backward when it came to women's voting rights. Social hierarchies that allow others to become invisible because of their color, gender, or station in life are cultural values. These misguided values have been used throughout history to justify social institutions such as slavery and the denial of women's rights.

However, before we are too quick to throw Christianity under the bus, we should note that many other religions have historically supported slavery as well, including but not limited to Islam, Hinduism, and Buddhism.

"When bad things happen to men we say it's terrible, but when bad things happen to women we say that's just a cultural practice," says Lou de Baca, United States Ambassador-at-Large, Office to Combat and Monitor Human Trafficking.[9] Women and children constitute 80 percent of trafficking victims. Perhaps that's why modern slavery hasn't been challenged the way that it should.

The hard part about these judgments toward people is that we often make them unconsciously. I am probably the most nonhierarchical person I know, yet nearly every day I catch myself thinking a hierarchical thought. That's how deep the conditioning goes. Even being aware of our tendency to classify people according to some internal pecking order doesn't stop it. But we must continue to try. As we put aside the preconceived agendas and false belief systems that blind us to hierarchy, we begin to recognize slavery, as well as why it has been perpetuated.

Lately, however, I'm finding myself frequently asking a question: "If I'm to love my neighbor as myself, am I treating others the way I would want to be treated?" For me, this can be as simple as the challenge to leave the other person better than I found him or her. While that might sound easy or cliché, it requires a conscious effort each minute of the day.

Doing the Right Thing

I *can* do the things I know I'm supposed to do day by day, whether those are big things or just simple courtesies. That doesn't mean I have a perfect track record, but when I fail I'm reminded that "I'm sorry" may be two of the most important words ever spoken, and I'm encouraged to keep trying.

Challenging our hierarchical assumptions helps remove our blinders and accept those whose lives may not be what we would wish for our loved ones or ourselves. We sometimes make a point of not looking at the sex-trafficked individual with her short skirt and makeup who is probably carrying STDs, or at the stooped-over farmworker laboring in the field. We can find ourselves feeling uncomfortable because of their presence, and their needs make us not want to think about them. But these are the very people who are our neighbors.

Since I've started doing anti–human trafficking work, Christmas Eve has been a hard day for me. As I scurry around with my last-minute preparations for the big holiday, I can't help but think, "What about those being sexually exploited in a brothel tonight? What about the man who buys a sex slave tonight as a gift to himself for Christmas? And what about the woman he's buying? She is a real human being. Is she hiding tears of pain under a hard facade? Would she love nothing more than to be home with her family, but is too ashamed of what she's become to even call them?"

I would purport that protecting those who need to be protected, like those who are being trafficked, is part of loving others. No one in history better typifies this than Harriet Tubman.[10] Born into a Maryland slave family in the early 1820s, she carried scars on the back of her neck from the whippings she sustained as a child from the various masters for whom she worked. At age twelve, she refused to help tie up a slave who had tried to escape. The overseer threw a metal weight at Tubman, which hit her in the head. The skull fracture she sustained would cause her to live the rest of her life with her head drooped forward and her mouth often hanging open. She would fall asleep in the middle of things for no apparent reason and was regularly called "stupid."[11] To those who owned her, she was damaged, devalued property, not a person.

It was after she sustained the head injury that her faith became real to her. As an illiterate child, she heard Bible stories from her mother. Tubman acquired a passionate faith in God. She rejected the white people's interpretations of Scripture urging slaves to be obedient and justifying slavery as God-ordained; instead, Harriet found guidance in the Old Testament tales of deliverance.[12]

Harriet Tubman lived in minute-by-minute dependence on God throughout her life. Because of this, Tubman lived an example of a life of love and was able to value a person above her disagreements with them or even their abuse of her.

In 1849, she heard her Lord's voice warning her to flee northward.[13] Guided by the voice within her and narrowly escaping capture, she made good on her escape only to find herself alone and lonely for family and friends. There was no one to help her, none of her own folk to share her joy. Her entire family, everyone she knew, had remained behind in slavery. She made a promise to herself that she would make a home for her family in the North and help bring them to safety. "Oh, how I prayed then, lying on the cold, damp ground, 'Oh, dear Lord, I ain't got no friend but you. Come to my help, Lord, for I'm in trouble!'"[14]

She used her contacts and hard-won knowledge to bring others to freedom. Night and day she worked, saving pennies. When she had enough money, off she slipped from her home to rescue slaves and pilot them north. She returned to the South nineteen times, "bold to the point of brazenness," they said.[15] She delivered hundreds—and some say indirectly thousands—of slaves. She was so successful that a rumored $40,000 reward was offered for her capture, dead or alive.[16]

That was a huge sum in those days. But slavery then, as slavery now, is about money. And Harriet was really raising havoc with the slaveholders' wallets. Many times Tubman experienced a narrow escape. Always, she said, the Lord sent help. Once she had to lie wet in a swamp. Another time she had to bury herself in a potato field.[17] But deliverance always came, sometimes through a friend on the Underground Railway, sometimes through her own wits.

She experienced many narrow and harrowing escapes. As biographer Sarah Bradford wrote, "These sudden deliverances never seemed to strike her as at all strange or mysterious; her prayer was the prayer of faith, and she *expected* an answer. . . . When surprise was expressed at her courage and daring, or at her unexpected deliverances, she would always reply: 'Don't, I tell you, Missus, 'twan't *me*, 'twas *de Lord*!'"[18]

Her boldness to lead slaves out of slavery earned her the nickname "Moses,"[19] stemming from Exodus 25 in the Bible. She believed she had been called by God to help her people and once told an interviewer, "Now do you suppose he wanted me to do this just for a day or a week? No! The Lord who told me to take care of my people meant me to do it just so long as I live, and so I do what he told me to do."[20]

Though she was impoverished in her old age, her spirit remained unquenchable, and by her incredibly courageous actions in what she termed obedience, she changed the course of history. She was a person who dared to love her fellow human beings unconditionally, even when she could have paid for that love with her life.

Might I suggest that we follow in the path of this young girl who was often called "stupid"? A girl who had no choices about whose slave she was. She was willing to overcome any and all obstacles to obtain freedom for herself and others. She then used past obstacles as stepping-stones to facilitate freedom for many grateful souls. She was courageous and stepped out in faith, and she lived an extraordinary life because of it. She had a steadfast love for others and believed in the best for them.

For me, working to end modern slavery is not even a matter of fighting for rights for the disenfranchised, but rather for righteousness. This is the right thing to do. What can I do today to help bring modern slavery to an end?

What about You?

Have you been called to join in the battle, even in what you might consider a small way? If so, then it's time to get involved in the fight—today!

When she took Given Kachepa into her home after his atrocious experience with the boys' choir, Sandy Shepherd knew in her heart that it was the right thing to do. She had every reason to believe that she wasn't the right person to help bring Given a life of freedom and the opportunity to develop his full potential. But it turns out she was the perfect person for the job.

As clearly demonstrated throughout history, the chosen vessels of change are men and women, people who see what needs to be changed and who summon the courage to speak up and do what needs to be done.

That held true during the abolitionist movements of the seventeenth through nineteenth centuries, and I believe it still holds true today. I believe we all have an obligation to recognize the suffering of modern-day slaves at the hands of human traffickers and slave masters, and that we can aid in their freedom in one way or another.

Fortunately, there is much that each of us can do to help, with little or no interruption or change to our lifestyles.

Speak Up!

There is nothing the criminals involved in the modern-day atrocities of human trafficking and slavery—the recruiters, the traffickers, the pimps—want more than for decent people to remain ignorant about what they do. All they ask is that we do nothing. Simple silence. If the myth that "it doesn't happen here" can prevail, they have won.

Knowing that, one answer to the question "What can I do?" is to look for opportunities to tell others about these horrible abuses against our fellow human beings. We can follow the historical example of Harriet Tubman and the modern-day example of Sandy Shepherd, both of whom courageously spoke out against the injustices they encountered. Follow the historic examples of John Wesley, William Wilberforce, and Sojourner Truth, who spoke out against the enslavement of fellow human beings during a time when people didn't want to hear what they had to say. I have vowed that as long as I have breath, I will speak of this atrocity.

If you become aware of a situation in which human trafficking could be involved, don't just sit by and wait for someone else to speak up or act. Notify your local authorities, call the National Human Trafficking Hotline at 1-888-373-7888, or text "HELP" to BeFree (233733). This hotline, which is toll-free and open twenty-four hours a day, is staffed by specialists who will help you determine if you have actually encountered a case of human trafficking, will identify resources available in your community to help victims, and will help you coordinate with local social service organizations to protect and serve victims so they can begin the process of restoring their lives. The website is http://www.acf.hhs.gov/trafficking/.

Your words may or may not make a huge dent in the modern slave trade, but they could very possibly save the life of someone's daughter or son.

For Discussion

1. Did Given's story of slavery happening right inside churches surprise you? How can we be wise against evil and yet gentle to those who need our compassion in matters such as this?

2. Can you think of other ways people could have spoken up to facilitate the freedom of Given and others who were trapped by TTT?

3. Harriet Tubman's life was one that had an impact on lives for generations to come. Is there something in her life that inspires you to take a stand against modern slavery? If so, what might you do to take that stand?

4. Can you speculate about why people of various religions have historically defended slavery?

5. Find a recent news story in which someone took action to stop modern slavery and discuss it.

3

From Farm to Factory

Where, after all, do universal human rights begin? In small places, close to home—so close and so small that they cannot be seen on any maps of the world. Yet they are the world of the individual person; the neighborhood he lives in; the school or college he attends; the factory, farm, or office where he works.

—Eleanor Roosevelt

Quyen Truong,[1] a Hawaiian resident in her early thirties, isn't ashamed to tell anyone who asks about how she lost her eye. "I tell everybody when they meet me," she says in her broken English. "I'm not ashamed. My experience—nothing to be ashamed."[2] In 1999, at age twenty-one, she had relocated from Vietnam to American Samoa with the promise of a sewing job that paid $408 a month. She needed funds to help support her younger sister and widowed mother in Vietnam and was hoping for a better life with more

63

money for herself as well as for her family. The video she'd been shown about the job at Daewoosa helped ease the pain of leaving them behind. She would live in spacious quarters, have access to a swimming pool, and be fed three nutritious meals a day.[3] What a contrast to the poverty that surrounded her in Vietnam.[4]

The buy-in was high. Neither Quyen nor her family had the $5,000 required[5] to secure the job and pay transportation expenses, but this was a chance to improve her life. Somehow she managed to scrape together the money. When she passed the sewing and fitness tests, she was thrilled. She could now fly to American Samoa and become part of a group of three hundred Vietnamese and Chinese workers making garments for companies such as Walmart, JC Penney, Sears, and Target.[6]

Her dreams dissolved the moment she entered the company's barbed wire compound and saw the grim, gray walls and the massive Samoan guards who didn't speak her language and carried sticks. She had been duped. The spacious room she had been promised turned out to be prison-like quarters, where thirty-six people were stuffed into a muggy hallway with minimal ventilation and bunk beds with half-inch-thick mattresses. The bathrooms had broken toilets. Instead of clear blue water, the swimming pool she had viewed on the video was green with slime that stank.[7]

As in so many human trafficking situations, Quyen and the other slaves were forced to work grueling hours and were fed just enough to keep them alive—in this case, minimal amounts of boiled potatoes, rice, and cabbage, with no meat.[8] Back in their mother country, even if they were poor they had rice cakes, along with meat and vegetable dishes on special occasions.[9]

By late 2000, Quyen had been labeled as a troublemaker at Daewoosa for objecting to the gruesome conditions and the lack of nutrition. She knew that her outspokenness could cost her. "You can beat anyone who don't listen to you," Daewoosa owner Kil

Soo Lee had told a Samoan supervisor when faced with a tough deadline on a big contract. "If anyone die, I will be responsible."[10] The workers understood all too clearly that production and the bottom line were more important than their lives. One slipup, one hint of disloyalty could prove deadly.

Lee had built his factory, located about 2,300 miles south of Honolulu, in unincorporated American Samoa.[11] The choice was no accident. The area is well known for its poor treatment of workers and pitifully low wages. Yet American Samoa is a territory of the United States, so despite its record of human rights violations, garments made there carry the "Made in the USA" label.[12] It doesn't matter that American citizens don't sew these garments. It doesn't matter that they're produced by skilled workers kept there by force (including sexual assault) and threats of arrest, deportation, and violence.

That wasn't Lee's only hold on the women. In addition to being charged from $4,000 to $8,000 to acquire their jobs—the equivalent of eight to fifteen years' salary in Vietnam or China—the workers were required to sign contracts that contained a three-year commitment and a $5,000 penalty for breaching that agreement.[13] Many of them had sold their homes and/or borrowed money from relatives or loan sharks to follow a dream that promised stability and financial gain. They had little to return to. Just to make sure they would continue to grow the company's profits, which totaled $8 million in 1999, Lee also confiscated the workers' passports and alien registration cards.[14]

Armed security guards enforced Lee's intimidation tactics in a compound that more closely resembled a penal complex than a factory. In November of 2000, Lee ordered his guards to attack any workers who tried to defy his authority[15] or who were working too slowly.[16] As the guard came toward Quyen with a length of PVC pipe, his thick arm ready to smash her body, the young woman knew she was in danger. The beating, which would literally and figuratively scar her for life, continued for what seemed like an eternity. She didn't think the pain could get any worse until her assailant raised the PVC pipe and poked it into her eye socket. She would lose her eye as a result.[17]

To this day, Quyen relives the experience. "It's like a movie that plays over and over, and I cannot stop it when it happens," she told the media after being rescued. "Injury to the body can be mended, but injury to the soul and mental being . . . what can a doctor do to treat you?"[18]

The workers were eventually rescued when one of the captives managed to toss an SOS note from the window of a company car. The note was found and passed along to the Department of Labor.[19]

The prosecution of Lee in 2003 on fourteen counts,[20] including holding workers in a condition of involuntary servitude and conspiring to violate civil rights, was at that time one of the biggest modern slavery cases in US history.[21] But it is far from the only one.

Products Made by Slave Labor?

Modern slaves are all around us. We unwittingly participate in their enslavement through acts as simple as buying manufactured products. From cell phones to fast food to clothing, so many of the companies we support with our dollars each day, week, month, and year sell goods produced at least in part by individuals who have been enslaved in the name of profit.

How do we know if the shirt we just purchased as a birthday gift—or the well-made slacks that are such a good buy—were made by a legitimate garment factory or by a place like the Samoan factory? The short answer is we usually can't be certain that a product doesn't have slave labor in its composition somewhere along the line. As illustrated in the above story, just because a product is marked "Made in America" doesn't guarantee it is not, at least partially, a result of slave labor.

Although the stories of individuals victimized by predators like Kil Soo Lee are distressing and far too numerous, a vast number of slave-made products come from China. The Chinese have found a way to convert some of their prisons into prison factories (called *Laojiao*), which incarcerate those the government feels are a threat to national security or considers unproductive. The practice has become lucrative business for China.

Conceptually, this may sound like a wise plan to keep the prison population busy in a constructive way that benefits their country. In China, however, a person can be arrested for disagreeing with the government or for participating in religious practices not sanctioned by the government. Charges may be something like "not engaging in honest pursuits" or "being able-bodied but refusing to work."[22] Those so charged are not entitled to the same judicial procedures as some other offenders and may be sent directly to prison via an administrative sentence by local public security forces. Additionally, due to Chinese governmental policies, 70 percent of prisoners are not released at the completion of their sentences but are held at the prison and must continue working there.[23]

Enslaved for Moral Convictions

The prison factory system of *Laogai* has become a way to deter and eliminate opposition groups, including those who oppose or criticize the government, are human rights activists,[24] practice Falun Gong, or have been part of Christian churches that fall outside the government church. Indeed, as shocking as it may sound, our regular buying habits may mean that we're supporting the slave labor of some courageous Chinese people who have been imprisoned for living out their moral convictions.[25]

While there are laws against importing slave-made products into the United States, the Chinese get around those laws because each *Laogai* camp has both a camp name and a public name. The Shanghai Municipal Prison, for example, is also referred to as the Shanghai Printing and Stationery Factory. In *Human Rights Brief*, Ramin Pejan writes, "Financial information on ninety-nine forced labor camp enterprises collected by Dunn and Bradstreet was released on June 30, 1999. According to this data, the ninety-nine camps had total annual sales of US $842.7 million. These camps represent only 9 percent of the roughly 1,100 known *Laogai* camps."[26] When the factories are discovered by the outside world, the Chinese government simply closes and moves them or reopens them under other names.

That is not to imply that all slave-made goods imported into the United States are from China, nor that all Chinese-made goods are from *Laogais*, but it is another example of how slave-made goods permeate our buying habits here in America.

Debt Bondage

Slavery in domestic agriculture—as well as in almost all other forms of human trafficking—usually includes the component of debt bondage. In this form of financial control and intimidation, the captor keeps a tab for all the victim's "expenses." These may include (but are not limited to) transportation costs for the victim to arrive at the place where he or she operates as a modern slave, food, shelter, clothing, tips paid, and anything else needed for everyday life. For those trapped in sex trafficking, expenses can also include manicures, makeup, hair styling, condoms, costumes, photo sessions, advertising, and protection.

In the best-case scenario, a worker in debt bondage ends up paying many times the amount he or she originally agreed to pay to acquire the job, or an inflated price for even valid charges. In the worst-case scenario, debt bondage becomes a tool captors use to keep their slaves imprisoned.

In short, the system is designed to keep slaves working harder than they've ever worked, harder than any human being should be required to work, and the slaveholder sees to it that the debt meets or exceeds the salary owed. Additionally, forcing slaves to purchase necessities in company stores with inflated markups helps ensure that victims may never be able to repay their escalating debt no matter how many hours they put in. According to evidence in the 1998 El Monte, California, sweatshop case, where seventy-two Thai garment workers were kept for eight years in slavery and debt bondage, the company store the workers were obliged to use charged $20 for a simple bar of soap.[27]

In Kevin Bales and Ron Soodalter's book *The Slave Next Door*, Lucas Benitez describes the process of enslavement:

> Debt begins when the coyote turns you over to the crew leader. So many of our compañeros have suffered in this way and say being sold . . . feels worse than being an animal. . . . You get sold for $500, but the next day the debt is $1,000. Then they add on rent and food, and your debt increases. . . . If you have a slow day in the fields, the crew leader will say "you owe us more now; you didn't work well." You never see the check stubs, so you have no idea where you stand with your debt.[28]

When victims finally become so weary of their living situation that they muster up the courage to ask their captor to set them free, they are told that they must first repay the debt they have incurred. This not only keeps victims enslaved, it allows the perpetrator to demand more and greater output from the slaves. Physical and psychological abuses inflicted on the slaves help cement those demands, as does the victims' hope that they will be able to pay off the debt if they just work hard enough. Ironically, that goal often diverts their thoughts from the truth of the matter: they are slaves and cannot leave without threat of physical harm or death.

How can this be happening in our very own country? Again, we have to look at our sense of hierarchy. I remember the caution from my parents as I was helping prepare fresh fruits and vegetables for dinner as a child. "Wash that carefully," they would tell me. "Remember, the last person to handle it was a migrant worker with *dirty* hands." That vision was enough for me to carefully scrub the tomato or apple, sometimes even with soap.

But who *are* these migrant workers with dirty hands? People of lesser value than those who live in our neighborhoods? Perhaps in the eyes of society they are. In reality, however, they are someone's mother or father, sister or brother, husband or wife, someone's child. And for those of us who believe in equality, they are certainly equals.

Antonio Martinez was what some would term a migrant worker. However, a closer look at his life reveals he could be more accurately described as a slave.[29]

In Hidalgo, Mexico, Antonio was the oldest of six children. He felt the responsibility to support his family because his parents were not in good health.[30] One day he met a contractor, also known as a *coyote*, who promised him construction work in California if Antonio would pay him some 16,000 pesos (about $1,700 in American dollars) to get across the border into the United States. That was a fortune to Antonio. He couldn't possibly earn—let alone save—a sum like that in Mexico. The *coyote* reassured him that paying the money back would be easy once Antonio had crossed the border and secured his construction job.[31]

Two weeks later, Antonio and more than three dozen other hopefuls boarded a bus to the land of opportunity. At the Sonoran Desert, the bus stopped and new *coyotes* took responsibility for the travelers. Antonio was placed in a group led by a man named Chino. For the next three days, Antonio and his group hiked across the hot, dry desert with just a single day of supplies.[32]

Hungry, thirsty, and exhausted, they finally crossed the border and were driven to a house in Tucson, Arizona. Instead of being fed and given a chance to rest, Chino ordered Antonio and the others to hand over more cash. Antonio was broke. He had nothing. The ensuing threats of violence made him realize just how helpless he'd suddenly become. But there was no turning back now. He had no funds and no documentation. He was at the *coyote*'s mercy.[33]

Then came what must have sounded like good news. Although Antonio wouldn't be given the promised construction job in California, he would be sent to Florida to make $150 a day in the tomato fields.[34] That was a lot of money! His momentary sense of hope, however, proved false.

Chino turned Antonio and seventeen other Mexican workers over to a van driver called El Chacal—the jackal—who crammed them all into the back of a van and made them sit on the floor to escape the authorities' notice.[35] For four days, the van only stopped for gasoline. Even then, its passengers were not allowed to get out. As documented later in a criminal report by senior patrol agent Jose M. Lopez of US Immigration, "During the trip, the men in the group were made to urinate in plastic jugs, and the woman . . . did not urinate until two days into the trip, when the van had to stop to repair a flat tire, because she was unable to use the jug."[36] Although the eighteen migrants who had to share the floor of the van for four long days were given just two bags of chips to share during the entire trip to Florida, each was charged $700 for transportation and food, to be paid in hard labor.[37]

Upon his arrival in South Florida, Antonio and the other workers who had been crammed into the back of the van were taken to a labor camp run by Abel and Basilio Cuello.[38] Any lingering expectations about improving his situation evaporated when Antonio heard El Chacal and the Cuellos haggling over his price tag. El Chacal was demanding $500 for him and for each of the other migrants, and the Cuellos were offering $350 each. "We were being sold like animals," Antonio recalls.[39]

The migrants worked long, hard hours in the field. The way the debt and wages were structured, however, made it virtually impossible to repay the amount they supposedly owed and free themselves from the debt bondage that enslaved them.

They were housed in a mobile home at 1365 Sanctuary Road in Immokalee, Florida.[40] That home on Sanctuary Road was anything but a sanctuary, with mattresses on the floor and only four or five dishes to share the inadequate meals that left them feeling hungry. "I thought I was going to die there, because I didn't eat well," Antonio recalls.[41] There were roaches everywhere and holes in the floor, exposing snakes below. One of Antonio's co-workers awoke one night with a scorpion sting on his neck.[42]

Worse than the grim conditions, Antonio and the two dozen others who were stuffed into the small mobile home couldn't leave. The Cuellos made sure of that by locking them in at night. Abel Cuello would show up in the morning to unbolt the door and drive them to the fields.[43] This daily transportation to the fields where they were enslaved was charged against their wages, along with rent for their nightly prison, the scant amounts of food they were fed, and the foul water that was supplied.[44] Workers used the small amount of salary they had left to purchase toiletries and food on those infrequent occasions when their captors took them to a small nearby grocery.[45]

An opportunity to escape presented itself when, during one of those rare outings to the store, Cuello fell asleep while standing guard outside. Despite threats of violence should they try to flee,[46] when Antonio and the others saw him napping, they seized their chance and raced to the highway and eventually to safety.[47]

"For four and a half months, I was held in forced labor in the fields against my will, and it seemed like an eternity for me," Antonio says. "They were watching me all the time, controlling all I did. I thought I was going to die. Thanks to God I was able to escape, and it allowed me to become more aware. I'm out here learning more every day."[48]

Cuello pleaded guilty to one count of involuntary servitude. In 1999, he was sentenced to thirty-three months in prison. Two of his relatives, who were co-defendants, were also convicted.[49] Before Cuello went to prison, he spotted Antonio and gave chase in his Chevy Suburban, demanding his *coyote* fee back and swearing at the top of his lungs.[50] According to the *Miami Herald*, Cuello has since created another harvesting company based in Naples, Florida.[51]

Antislavery advocates believe there are many, many male and female slaves working in our fields and factories. Indeed, the numbers are so high that these slave-based operations often remain undetected. Meanwhile, the personal tragedies continue to mount.

In 1999, a young Guatemalan woman by the name of Maria Choz was forced to come to this country when native Guatemalan José Tecum, who owned the largest home in their community, threatened to kill Maria or her father if she wasn't given to him. Tecum then smuggled Maria into the United States.[52]

Authorities responded to a domestic call at Tecum's home in Immokalee, Florida. Officers observed that Maria "cried and visibly shook."[53] She said she was required to do whatever Tecum ordered— including servicing him sexually—and that she considered herself a slave. Her labor for Tecum included work at a local farm. During the trial, the prosecutor nailed Tecum, saying, "Every paycheck she earned, he took it. And she received maybe one or two or three dollars."[54]

Maria's response in court reminds me of so many other survivors. "I don't want to look at his face," she responded when prosecutors requested that she identify Tecum.[55] Fear, shame, and pain often prompt such a response. Victims and survivors innately know they never deserved to be treated as subhuman beings in the first place, but sorting that out in their hearts, lives, and minds is a process that takes many years and sometimes is never achieved.

Tap the Power of the Purse

Slave-produced products are all around us, from garments labeled "Made in the USA" but sewn by slaves, to products made by those imprisoned in China for their faith, to the food that we eat every day. Other goods tainted by the slave trade include cell phones, automobiles, jewelry, cosmetics, electronics, sports equipment, rugs, and agricultural products such as tomatoes, sugar, tea, coffee, chocolate, and seafood.

How can we help solve this important matter? As we all become more aware and bring awareness to those around us, we can each help break the chain of slavery within the products we use every day. That doesn't mean boycotting an entire industry, which is often the concerned consumer's knee-jerk reaction. Just as not all goods coming from China are made by slaves, not all of any one product is slave-made. In fact, even in products known to be contaminated by slavery, such as chocolate or diamonds or tomatoes, only a small percentage of those products utilizes slave labor in its manufacture and delivery. So if we boycott the purchase of all chocolate, diamonds, or tomatoes, we hurt the vast majority of those supplying slavery-free products in return for a fair profit.

A 2010 documentary titled *The Dark Side of Chocolate* tells the secrets behind child slavery in the Ivory Coast. Children between the ages of eleven and fifteen are coerced or kidnapped from their homes. The men who worked undercover to make the documentary filmed one trafficker telling plantation owners that he could supply them with children for labor for about 230 euros each (that was his price before the typical bargaining ensued). Included in the price was transport and delivery of the children to their buyer, who would have indefinite use of each child for whatever purposes they chose.

Traffickers are motivated by money. By cutting off their income stream, we can stop slavery at its root. We can affect their profits by requesting fair-trade items and informing those around us about the need for fair trade. Tragedies like the kidnapping and enslavement of children on the Ivory Coast will only be averted by taking away the demand and profitability.

Demand Fair-Trade Products

So what can you and I do as consumers? We can insist on fair-trade products. Purchasing fair-trade products is one of the best and safest ways to ensure that the goods we purchase are not tainted with slavery. After being informed by that documentary, I have pledged to buy only fair-trade chocolate products. I can't in good conscience eat chocolate when, in my mind, I see enslaved children. While my efforts don't in and of themselves solve the problem, I know each small piece and each individual consumer is important in the puzzle.

A unique business model for fair-trade products brings together producers and buyers with the common goal of creating a sustainable living wage for those involved with a product's production. Buyers and producers work in cooperation, adhering to a set of fair-trade criteria established by the International Fair Trade Association for handicrafts or the Fair Trade Labeling Organization for agricultural commodities. The criteria include fair wages, good working conditions, safety procedures, and adequate health standards for all workers. Producers also agree to adhere to environmentally sound production methods. Finally, buyers and producers must also promote human rights, especially the rights of the disenfranchised—women, children, and those with disabilities.[56]

When the opportunity arises, buying fair-trade items ensures that the product was not produced with slave labor. But fair-trade products aren't always available. That's where you can make an active difference. Take time to go to the store manager and ask about a product. Politely state that fair-trade items that do not contain slavery in their production line are important to you, and ask the manager to make the appropriate calls to ensure that no slavery taints the product. He or she may or may not be able to give you the information you need. Even so, you'll have alerted the manager to the fact that selling fair-trade items is important to a sector of their customers. That will influence their future buying decisions. And we all know how loudly money talks.

Some of the world's brightest individuals have joined in the fight against slavery, so stay tuned to this movement. Universities and scholars are beginning new research studies every day that will empower abolitionists to better engage in the fight against human trafficking. Technology companies such as Microsoft, Apple, and Google are developing ways to locate and report suspected slavery within the tech world. Outside-of-the-box ideas are needed to track the supply line for products available.

In 2012 California enacted laws that mandate transparency for some larger businesses in an attempt to eliminate human trafficking in their supply chains. These laws pertain to labor performed in the state of California and also to sweatshops or child labor in other countries.

It remains to be seen how effective such laws will be in fighting human trafficking. The good news is that we are seeing more and more attempts to fight human trafficking, not just by increased awareness but by laws that can effect change and give law enforcement and other government officials the tools they need to crack down on traffickers.

Recently I was in a gathering of law enforcement personnel who were discussing how they could interrupt the human trafficking that they knew was occurring in their jurisdiction. One officer brought to the meeting a recent statute that we worked to pass in the last legislative session. It contains a small clause that would enable them to arrest sex buyers for certain acts if they were performed in strip clubs. The group was pleased to understand the implementation of this new law and to have it in their "toolbox" to arrest perpetrators and give victims of sex trafficking opportunities to exit their enslavement.

Getting behind and initiating effective new human trafficking legislation is one practical way regular citizens can stop human trafficking. In 2013 I had an idea for a new law in my state of Oregon that would, among other things, amend Oregon's Trafficking in Persons Act to specifically address sex trafficking of both adults and children, eliminating the defense that a sex buyer didn't know the real age of a victim, and to provide compensation for medical bills and other related expenses. I went to my local senator and asked him to write a bill based on a new law that had just been passed in the state of Louisiana. He was pleased to do so, and after many phone calls, written communications, and significant research on my part, "my" bill dropped on the floor of the state senate and I began to learn about politics at a state level. Some of the lessons I learned were interesting and even a little fun; others were shocking and disappointing. Such is politics, but it is certainly a vehicle by which we can effect widespread and long-lasting change.

In the end, my bill was combined with a bill drafted by another nonprofit, and it was then passed into law in July of 2013. We didn't get everything we wanted, which I learned takes time and a lot of hard work, but we are working toward that end. The daughters and sons who are being cruelly enslaved, beaten, raped, and tortured—in both sex trafficking and labor trafficking, in our state and others—deserve to have us fight for them. Law enforcement and prosecutors need practical tools in the form of laws that will enable them to not only arrest traffickers but also administer justice in the form of strict sentences for human trafficking.

As citizens and as consumers, we hold powerful tools in our hands: money and votes. Using those wisely will help us end modern slavery.

For Discussion

1. Is it surprising to you that an item labeled "Made in America" could have slave labor in its chain of manufacturing or delivery? Why are items labeled "fair trade" important in our purchasing decisions?

2. Explain how the *Laojiao* system works in China. If we purchase products from a *Laojiao*, how might we actually be supporting religious persecution in China?

3. What is debt bondage? How does it assist traffickers in keeping their victims enslaved? Does it affect sex trafficking in different ways than it affects labor trafficking?

4. Not all migrant workers are slaves. What is the difference between a migrant worker who is a slave and one who is simply working crops for a fair wage?

5. How can boycotting a particular product, such as cocoa, harm those who are not involved with human trafficking?

6. Find a labor trafficking case in the news and discuss it. How could that case affect your buying choices?

4

Just the Help

> Slavery is one of those monsters of darkness to whom the light of truth is death.
>
> —Frederick Douglass

Slavery is clearly woven into each of our lives. It doesn't just lie hidden on farms and in factories. In too many cases, you don't have to look any farther than your own neighborhood—yes, your own backyard—to find modern slaves.

Tina Font didn't react when she began to spot the same slender, dark-haired young girl in her neighbor's house doing dishes night after night at 10:00 p.m., 11:00 p.m., and even as late as midnight. "We didn't put two and two together," the Irvine, California, resident says.[1] Neighbors like Font had no way of knowing that thirteen-year-old Shyima Hall had already spent three years being forced to work up to twenty hours a day for the Egyptian couple who had purchased her from her parents a year before coming to the United States.[2]

While other children were at school, Shyima, who stood not much taller than the countertop where she washed the dishes, was forced to do the family's laundry and ironing, get the children ready for school (including one girl her own age), cook their food, and clean the inside and outside of their lavish Tuscan-style home, including mopping the marble floors and dusting the crystal chandeliers.

Instead of joining the family for meals, Shyima ate alone. At every turn, she was made to feel that she was less than the other family members. "They called me stupid girl," she recalls.[3] That's when they called her anything at all.

After her grueling twenty-hour workdays, the tiny girl would finally collapse on a filthy, bare mattress in the windowless garage, which was neither air-conditioned nor heated. She lived there in darkness, since the only lightbulb had burned out shortly after her arrival and was never replaced. Shyima's captors even demanded that she do her own laundry in a bucket by her mattress, saying that her clothes were too dirty for the washing machine.[4]

Still, Shyima never considered running away. "I thought this was normal," she says.[5] She would scarcely have had the chance even if she had wanted to flee, since she was never allowed outside the family house unaccompanied. Besides, she had been repeatedly threatened that if she told anyone about her situation, the police would come and take her away because she was in the country illegally.[6]

Finally, someone did notice that something wasn't right. On April 9, 2002, an anonymous call, probably from a neighbor, alerted authorities that a young girl who seemed to be a maid rather than a member of the family was living in the garage and not attending school. When an Orange County Child Protective Services social worker responded, the sight of Shyima's shabby brown T-shirt, baggy pants, and raw, red hands told her what she needed to know. When Shyima, through a translator, confirmed that she hadn't attended school during the two years she'd been in the United States, she was taken into protective custody, and the husband and wife who had enslaved her were arrested and charged with involuntary servitude, obtaining the labor of another person illegally, conspiracy, and harboring an alien.[7]

During their 2006 trial, the couple argued that Shyima had been a member of the family. She even accompanied them on a trip to Disneyland, they told the court. They neglected to add that she had been there only to carry the family's bags and had not been allowed to go on any rides.[8] Shyima broke down. "Where was their loving when it came to me?" she told the court, unable to hold back her sobs. "Wasn't I a human being, too? I felt like I was nothing when I was with them."[9]

After years of therapy and three foster homes, Shyima, now in her twenties, is stable and strong and has finally found a family, a life, a cause, and a dream. She and her boyfriend are proud parents of a beautiful little girl, and Shyima works to make a living.[10] She's determined to become a United States Immigration and Customs Enforcement (ICE) agent like Mark Abend, the ICE supervisory special agent who headed up the investigation that led to her captors' conviction. In the meantime, she speaks publicly about her plight and the need for people to keep their eyes open, stressing that human trafficking happens in even the most affluent communities. "Take your chances," she told one group gathered to hear about her experience and learn how to prevent human trafficking. "You might just save somebody's life."[11]

For more details on her story, I recommend Shyima's book *Hidden Girl: The True Story of a Modern-Day Child Slave*, a passionate and impressive account that documents her plight and courage.[12] It's a reminder to us all about the harsh reality of child labor trafficking in our country.

Sold—or Hoodwinked—into Slavery

Shyima is one of the 14,500 to 17,500 people trafficked into the United States every year.[13] In Egypt, as in many African countries, it is a common—albeit illegal—practice for destitute families to sell their children in order to make ends meet.

Although some human trafficking victims like Shyima are sold into slavery or kidnapped, the majority are tricked into going with their trafficker. They think they will be doing something different from the life of slavery in which they become trapped. Non-US victims are often told that they will be provided with a visa and a job, which will allow them to send funds back to their impoverished families staying behind. Once the victim has been duped or coerced into coming to this country with the trafficker, promises are broken and the game is changed. And what the victim may have thought was the opportunity of a lifetime becomes a nightmare.

When Charito,*[14] a stunningly beautiful thirty-two-year-old master chef working at a five-star hotel in Manila, read in the classifieds that an American-based Asian restaurant was looking for kitchen staff, she figured that the opportunity would be a good career move. The hotel had treated her very well, providing yearly bonuses as well as benefits. She loved her work and enjoyed her co-workers. She also loved her family—including her police officer father, stay-at-home mother, and two brothers—with whom she lived. She would miss them all. But relocating to the United States would move her even higher up the career ladder and provide a better lifestyle as well.

Charito had heard of the land of plenty in America. This was exactly the next step she needed. She would get to travel, learn new things, meet new people, and she would earn enough money to visit her family in the Philippines regularly. She had no reason to believe that she wouldn't be treated fairly. She had always treated others fairly and found people usually treated her well in return.

The restaurant interviewed fifty applicants and offered positions to just two—Charito and one other woman. Charito's tremendous excitement about being picked, however, was tempered by having to say good-bye to her family. She knew with her dad's poor health, her parents would never be able to visit her. It would be up to her to get back to the Philippines to see them.

When her plane landed in the United States, people from the restaurant met her as she came out of customs. As they shuffled her and the other young woman into the van, she was in awe of the American cities and the countryside they passed during the three-hour drive to her new home.

The very next day, she was presented with a contract that would bind her to her new employer for several years, with large penalties if she broke the contract. She had no option. She had to sign.

As soon as she began work, she knew something wasn't right. Her gruff and demanding new boss was impossible to please no matter how hard she worked. The first day was as long as the work was difficult. Charito started at 9:00 a.m. before the restaurant opened. Hours of chopping vegetables, chicken, and other meat was hard work. When it came time for her lunch break, she was allowed to eat only the fat and skin trimmed off the chicken as well as the stems of mushrooms and spinach and other waste. Between the jetlag from the trip, the long hours, and the lack of food, she soon became absolutely exhausted. But she continued to work for an hour after the restaurant closed at 10:00 p.m. Then, after fourteen unrelenting hours, she was told that she had not finished her work and would have to pack up some of the carrots and make them into little flowers while she was home that evening.

The next day was much the same, except that Charito, whose nature had always been loving and friendly, was reprimanded for talking with her co-workers. Charito had always quietly sung while she cooked and worked in the kitchen, but management forbade that too, along with any other noises deemed unnecessary for the work. Even laughing was prohibited. Her boss also advised her that there would be stiff penalties if she was caught talking to Americans, whether at the restaurant, on her way home, or wherever else she happened to be.

Physical, Mental, and Emotional Damage

Only after Charito had worked for a full week was she finally given a day off. She moved into a very small apartment that she shared with a co-worker. They weren't there much, because the majority of their time was spent slaving away at the restaurant.

The restaurant was staffed by Americans and Mexicans who were paid by the hour and Asian individuals on salary. Naturally, the bulk of the work went to the Asian workers who were paid the least, which netted higher profits for the restaurant. So Charito and her compatriots were required to labor however many hours it took to complete their tasks, which seemingly never ended. They worked in the restaurant six days a week, anywhere from twelve to fifteen hours a day. And just as she had the first day, Charito had to take home unfinished tasks as well.

Working in such a demanding and rigid environment would have been bad enough, but she was also subjected to emotional abuse. Fear, the restaurant management believed, would prompt their workers to perform better. Charito was regularly yelled at in front of others, including customers, and was told that she was stupid and ugly. When she wasn't being berated for nearly everything she did, Charito, along with the other Asian workers, was the brunt of nasty jokes, which proved particularly humiliating.

"People look at me like I steal money or something," she recalled. "I was so embarrassed."

When Charito's manager noticed a customer's concern during one such tirade, she cradled Charito's chin like a caring, loving friend and said, "I just care so much about you and I worry for you because you're a liar. You shouldn't do things like that. You're a liar." The demeaning words further damaged Charito, especially since they led the customer to believe that she was a lying and ungrateful employee.

The emotional trauma she experienced would erase childhood memories—from favorite songs to the name of her first school—from her mind. When she finally began to remember those details a couple of years after escaping the job, she felt like she was coming to life again. She felt she was luckier than another Asian worker at the restaurant who according to Charito, "completely lost his mind" due to the harsh psychological treatment. "He walk around like a tree, walked around everywhere and say nothing to anyone."

The disrespect Charito had to contend with didn't just come from the owners and the managers. The male Mexican workers would touch her bottom as they walked by. When she called them on it, they always told her it was an accident, but she knew better. All the Asian women who worked at the restaurant were being groped. When she complained to the owner, she was told, "You know you're not a beauty queen, you're not Miss USA, you're not a famous model. Why would they want to touch your bottom? You know you're not a star, they wouldn't even want to touch you." It became obvious that the men were allowed to sexually harass her and others, and neither she nor the other Asian women working there had any recourse.

The stress and grueling schedule quickly began to wear on her. After just a few months, Charito would look in the mirror when she got home and say to herself that she looked ten years older than she had when she left the Philippines. Shortly thereafter, she began to lose her hair. Thankfully, the kitchen hat she was required to wear at work spared her the embarrassment of being seen in that condition. Her hands would go next, victims of carpal tunnel syndrome that stemmed from the days and nights of long hours of strenuous repetitive motions.

Charito was not used to being mistreated, so she complained to the owner. "Party's over. Go home," the owner told her. "But first pay me six thousand dollars; you signed a contract." He added that the restaurant had control over her work visa. "In a dispute, the government will believe us, not you, because we're a big and powerful American restaurant." Charito felt she had nowhere to turn.

The Price of Defiance

A short time later, the owner, whom Charito had originally approached with her grievances, wandered back to the kitchen where Charito was slaving away. As he casually walked by her, he said, "If you go back to the Philippines and I see you on the sidewalk, you might want to be careful. An accident could happen to you." The threat was clear and only slightly veiled. Charito's life was in danger unless she complied with all her employer was requiring of her.

After two years, someone finally reported the restaurant to the Labor Bureau. Agency investigators eventually determined that the Asian people were being undercompensated and that the number of hours they were working was far beyond what was allowed by law.

"Did things get better then?" I asked Charito when I interviewed her.

"No. Then we had to punch in. We worked forty hours a week, plus ten hours overtime, and we punched out. But we were forced to work just as many hours as before and still had to take work home and were not paid for any of it."

To make matters worse, in addition to working the same long hours and continuing to take extra work home, the restaurant *cut* Charito's pay by about 25 percent.

Finally, she had taken all she thought she could possibly endure. After another public humiliation, numb from the painful exhaustion permeating her body and her now severely injured hands and arms, Charito walked out the door.

"I walked home for several blocks in the rain," she says. When she got back to her apartment, she didn't even have the strength or motivation to change into dry clothes. "I sat in the corner of the room in my apartment, curled up in a ball, and cried and cried until I fell asleep." The sleep didn't last long. All too soon, she heard people sent by her manager calling for her outside her window. She didn't feel like talking to anyone, and she knew whatever they said would not be pleasant. She couldn't take any more of their demoralizing and carefully crafted degradation, so she remained curled up in the corner of her apartment. In response, she heard her window break as a rock sailed through and landed on the floor. She understood her employer's wordless message: "We are watching you. You won't get away with this."

"I was so afraid, I didn't want to touch the curtain," says Charito. "I was too scared to move. I was cold and all my body shake, and they call, call, call, call. I'm crying and I'm sleeping, I sleep in the corner, all my body wet and dirty. And I kept thinking, 'This is not right, this is America, this is not right.'"

The next day she got up, showered, and went to work. One look at her manager, and she bolted. The manager grabbed her and physically restrained her. "I couldn't talk, like there was something

stuck in my throat and I cry," says Charito. "I want to run and lots
of people looked at me." Charito tried to get away, but the manager
took her by the waist and pulled her closer, saying, "Oh, I was so
worried about you. You shouldn't do things like that; you'll hurt
yourself. You need to quit lying."

That terrifying experience was typical of the abusive humiliation
inflicted on Charito by her manager, and it added to her chronic
exhaustion and high stress. Meanwhile, Charito's carpal tunnel
syndrome worsened. She now could no longer grip a knife for
more than five minutes at a time. One of the servers encouraged
her to see a doctor, who immediately recognized the seriousness of
her physical condition. His note to Charito's employers stressed
that her duties had to be changed. So they put her to work in the
storeroom.

"I am five-foot-one and weigh 110 pounds. I was required to
haul in fifty-pound bags of rice," she recalled. "The restaurant
sometimes makes over a hundred thousand dollars in one weekend.
Think how much rice we served and how many rice bags must be
carried." When others tried to help her lift the heavy bags, the
management told them not to provide assistance and that she had
to do the work by herself. "This was my punishment for going to
the doctor for my hands and arms."

Getting Help

Four years after Charito had been brought to the United States
under false pretenses, the web that her employers had woven to trap
her finally began to unravel. The kind server who had insisted that
Charito get medical attention for her hands and arms introduced
her to a retired Filipino American police officer who became a
friend. On his birthday, Charito phoned him to wish him a happy

birthday. When he heard the *click*, *click*, *click* in the background, he asked her about the noise.

"Oh, I'm carving carrots for work while I'm on the phone."

He asked her if they were paying her additional salary for this extra work.

"No, I do this all the time. It's part of my work. If I don't complete my work at the restaurant I must bring it home."

The former police officer began to ask more questions and quickly figured out that things were not right. He called a member of the state's Human Trafficking Task Force, who in turn connected Charito with a contracted government agency that helps trafficking victims navigate their way to safety, as well as with an attorney who would finally be able to stand up to her employer and claim the rights she had coming to her. As soon as her employers got wind of her actions, Charito was fired.

Today, some years later, Charito is once again happy. She has had several surgeries to repair the damage to her hands and arms and still has more surgeries to come. She has moved to a new city and now works for a different restaurant. "My boss, he is so nice and so good. He says thank you to me for my hard work. He pays us fairly and even sometimes brings the staff corn dogs we can eat." She marvels at having her life back. "Before I made so little; I have no life, no car; I was going numb. I couldn't remember things—my first dog, my first car, nothing. Now I have everything I want. I have good job, they treat me and all their employees fairly and I have a car; I have lots and lots of very good friends. My life is very, very good." She has even saved enough money to return home to her family for a visit. She carefully prepared her paperwork so she could make the trip and return to her job here, abiding by the laws of the United States, where she is pleased to live. Her family still doesn't know what happened to her. She doesn't want them to worry about her.

It is obvious that this woman wasn't looking for a handout or a free ride but really just wanted the fair salary she had been promised for a fair day's work. Her employers were investigated but not tried for human trafficking. Due to technicalities, the charges never stuck.

As I listened to Charito during our interview, I didn't hear an ounce of resentment toward the restaurant owners and employees who had abused her so terribly. I didn't hear a bit of built-up anger or hope for vengeance. Instead, she stuck strongly to her statements about injustice and the hope that everyone would be treated fairly and appreciated. I thought to myself, *I could learn from her. She is a strong yet gentle woman.*

I asked Charito what I could have done to help her if I had been a customer patronizing the restaurant where she was enslaved. "Don't complain about the food," she said. Whenever that happened, the manager came back to her area, threw the food at her, and berated her unmercifully.

I said, "But what if I wanted to do more for you than that? How would I know if you were being trafficked?" She said that someone hearing the manager yelling at her and berating her might have called the National Human Trafficking Hotline (1-888-373-7888) or the head of the state Human Trafficking Task Force that eventually helped her. While one report of a worker being yelled at won't necessarily trigger an investigation, repeated reports of suspected abuse must be investigated and may result in obtaining the help a worker needs before it is too late.

Importing Slaves to the United States

What happened to Charito is all too common. Convincing foreign nationals to come to the United States, where they think they'll make enough money to better their own lives and even be able to send cash back to the families they leave behind, is so easy that un-scrupulous individuals have turned it into big business. Thousands of people who leave their homeland for a better life for themselves and their families are funneled into employment agencies and hired out to major hotel chains, country clubs, resorts, and businesses to fill housekeeping, kitchen, landscaping, janitorial, maintenance, and roofing jobs, or any other duties that can be contracted out.

A trafficker's sales pitch to a company sounds as appealing as their pitch to the foreign national. It goes something like this: "We can bring in laborers for your company at less expense to you than if you hire them yourself. We do the hiring, firing, cover liability and other insurances, and look after any problems. Our employees work hard, and their oversight is our problem, not yours. You save money not only on salaries but also on labor disputes, liabilities, and supervisory staff."

What is a seemingly good deal for the hiring entity is a disaster for the laborers. For starters, they're housed in generally small, overcrowded facilities with little to no furniture. They're lucky to get an old mattress; often they sleep on the bare floor. Generally, each worker in the mixed-gender units is charged about half the total rent. With several workers in each unit, that amounts to a hefty profit for the criminal enterprise that enslaves them. The agency oversees all the workers' mail, ensuring that documents are filled out in ways that benefit the agency. All other communication is restricted as well. Because the laborers come into the country on work visas that then expire, those who try to secure alternative housing are quickly intimidated by assertions from their employer that their immigrant status will be revoked and the authorities will then bring legal consequences against them.

To further tighten the hold on their labor pool, agencies keep the workers in debt bondage, which we read about in chapter 3. The laborers are paid much less than what was promised, and the expenses the agency holds over their heads often add up to more than the workers could ever earn. Workers, however, are not allowed to seek other employment without paying the agency large sums of cash to buy out their contracts. So purchasing a plane ticket home or paying for their own living expenses while in the United States becomes a financial impossibility. They're stuck.

Threats of physical harm against these foreign nationals, as well as against their friends and family both in the United States and in their home country, further ensure cooperation with their trafficker, however involuntary. Randomly carrying out such a threat when someone doesn't comply with agency mandates is another brutally effective tool for keeping the laborers under the traffickers' control.

Recent large indictments against several employee-contracting agencies have helped spotlight these criminal operations. One indictment stated that the agency had failed to provide a proper salary or overtime pay and failed to pay the workers in a manner set forth in the terms of their contracts.[15] The company disregarded employment regulations and laws, and defrauded insurance companies in order to obtain the required coverage for their employed foreign nationals illegally working in the United States. Is it any wonder that an agency with so few scruples would likewise disrespect United States employment laws?

Still, too many of us remain unaware of these illegal agency operations. That, however, was certainly not true of Maria Alvarez,* the lively housekeeper who came in to clean my Denver hotel room during a recent trip.[16] After making small talk designed to ascertain whether she was safe and working under acceptable conditions, I asked if she worked directly for the hotel or for an agency. She announced with pride and conviction that she works only for the hotel directly. She went on to tell of others she knew who had been scammed by agencies. "I'm smarter than that," she said. She had learned what to look out for after friends and relatives had been duped.

Maria knew so much more than most of us who aren't aware of the problem and don't even realize that we may come into regular contact with people who have been trafficked. As I began meeting domestic slaves through my work with victims, I would take them to places like grocery stores or restaurants, only to find out that they had been in those exact locations with their slaveholders. As a result, I have come to realize that when doing our daily errands, we all could be standing in line next to a slave, someone we don't even notice because he or she is either quiet, shy, of a different culture, or speaks little to no English. So I have learned to keep an eye out and think past language barriers or self-protective postures when I suspect I am encountering a house slave. Most likely, the person in forced servitude doesn't even know that the people who keep her imprisoned in this job are not employers but slaveholders and human traffickers—aka criminals—and that she is a victim of modern slavery.

Conned, Intimidated, Coerced

The human trafficking dynamic parallels that of domestic violence in a multitude of ways. First, the perpetrator begins wooing the victim—and there's no one more charming than a person who is willing to ultimately try to control his or her victim through physical and emotional abuse. Even those perpetrators who aren't particularly charming don't initiate the discussion by overtly saying, "Hey, I'm going to beat the tar out of you if you don't do what I want." A domestic violence perpetrator comes to you and says in essence, "You are the most beautiful thing I have ever seen, and I really need you. I want to be a part of your life. I'd die if I couldn't have you. We can build a beautiful life together." Likewise, the trafficker woos the victim with flattery, promises, and hopes for the future.

Whether trafficking victims are duped, intimidated, or forced into slavery as servants, laborers, or prostituted people, they suffer similar circumstances: they're overworked, underpaid, deprived of food and medical attention, sometimes raped, and often beaten and physically abused in a myriad of ways.

What a victim gets or doesn't get hinges on the needs of the trafficker. Slaves are often provided with the cheapest food possible that may even be rancid, and only enough to keep them alive so they can continue to work. There's no compassion. Decisions about how to treat slaves revolve around the traffickers' needs rather than the slaves'. If it is to the slaveholder's advantage that the person in forced servitude not have decent clothing to wear out in public, then the victim will be shabbily dressed. If that slaveholder benefits from having somebody who blends in, then the victim will wear nice apparel, but those clothes will usually be charged against the victim's wages at a rate much higher than the actual price. This prevalent tactic of debt bondage works to keep all kinds of trafficking victims enslaved.

Though it is most commonly US citizens who wind up being sex-trafficked in America, those who are trafficked for labor more often come from other cultures. Their language barrier compounds their deprivation and isolation. This verbal obstacle makes asking for help especially difficult once they realize their forced servitude is unjust.

Additionally, a seemingly inescapable sense of hierarchy and preconceptions prevent us from recognizing that a problem exists. Instead of focusing on a fellow human being in front of us, we focus on their differences. They're just the help. So we look right past them and never notice the person or the crime of trafficking that's often happening in plain sight.

Still, some people do see what the rest of us don't. Of the small number of slaves freed in the United States each year, an estimated one-third are delivered from forced servitude because someone just like you or me noticed something that didn't look right and reported it instead of walking away.[17] Those of us working in anti-trafficking efforts believe that increased awareness can increase that number drastically.

The combination of high profits and low risk makes trafficking the fastest-growing criminal industry in the world, now second in size only to drugs. In 2014 the International Labor Organization (ILO) released an astounding report that estimated victims of human trafficking generate $150 billion of profit every year, with $99 billion in the sex industry and $51 billion in other sectors. These billions of dollars are generated off the backs of victims who need to be given freedom and a voice.

And as we've seen, it takes a pittance to keep a slave alive. The start-up costs for trafficking are extremely low. Traffickers are willing to use people and exploit any vulnerability with total disregard for how that may negatively affect the person they are trafficking. The willingness of a trafficker to use people as just an object from which to derive profit, combined with the immense demand for cheap labor or commercial sex, is a perfect storm for trafficking.

Traffickers count on us not seeing, and if we do notice something unusual, they hope we will mind our own business and not report it. Let's not empower traffickers. When we see something that could be human trafficking, let's report it to 1-888-373-7888 or text "HELP" to BeFree (233733).

Learn to Recognize the Stench of Human Trafficking

Anyone—no matter who they are or where they live—can fall victim to human trafficking. Take time to become educated on the subject so you'll know it when you see it. Watch a movie about human trafficking or modern slavery. One such movie, *Human Trafficking* (2005), starring Mira Sorvino and Donald Sutherland, was key in my decision to write this book. Spend fifteen minutes researching modern slavery online. Again, kudos to you for reading this book; you are taking a good step toward beginning to understand this atrocity.

Learn how to spot the signs of human trafficking. Read books or other publications on the subject, research it on the internet, or subscribe to a newsletter of an organization that combats human trafficking.

The appendix to this book provides information from the Polaris Project to help identify trafficking victims (see page 219). These potential indicators include observing poor or restrictive working conditions, poor mental health or abnormal behavior, poor physical health, lack of control, and inconsistencies in the person's story. If you see any of these red flags, call the National Human Trafficking Hotline at 1-888-373-7888 or text "HELP" to BeFree (233733) to report the situation.

When and if you do ask questions to determine whether someone is being trafficked, remember to exercise extreme caution. If you converse with someone you suspect is a victim, do it with great discretion and sensitivity, and *only* if she or he is alone. Asking questions in the presence of a trafficker could endanger both the victim's life and yours, and even though it may not be obvious, victims of human trafficking are constantly watched. Keep in mind, however, that a person truly being held in a trafficking situation will likely be unable or unwilling to answer your questions directly or at all due to fear caused by the treatment or trauma they have endured while enslaved. That fear could also stem from threats of retribution against their friends or family, as well as from despair over a perceived sense that nothing will ever change. Additionally, a victim of human trafficking is often extremely loyal to their captor because of a condition called traumatic bonding, which we will discuss more in chapter 8.

The Rescue & Restore Campaign of the US Department of Health and Human Services offers the following questions to help identify trafficking victims.[18] You may not be able to ask a suspected victim these questions directly, but such information will help determine whether you're dealing with a trafficking victim. Please remember that asking a trafficking victim the right questions at the wrong time, or even the wrong questions at the right time, can cost you and the trafficking victim your lives.

- What type of work do you do?
- Are you being paid?
- Can you leave your job if you want to?
- Can you come and go as you please?
- Have you or your family been threatened?
- What are your working and living conditions like?
- Where do you sleep and eat?
- Do you have to ask permission to eat/sleep/go to the bathroom?
- Are there locks on the doors/windows so you cannot get out?
- Has your identification or documentation been taken from you?

Please note: It is important to talk to potential victims in a safe and confidential environment. If someone accompanies the victim, discreetly attempt to separate the person from the individual accompanying him or her, since this person could be the trafficker. If they are unwilling or their "companion" is unwilling to separate from them, simply gather all the information you can, including description, exact location they were seen, license plates, and any other information. If it is a dangerous situation that is in progress, call 911 with this information.

Do not ask more questions of the victim or the trafficker than is socially acceptable. Mental health professionals, law enforcement professionals, or legal experts should be the ones conducting in-depth interviews with the possible victim. Even if your interaction with the victim is safe, unnecessary or inappropriate questions can revictimize them and cause unintentional trauma.

For Discussion

1. Why is it not necessarily better for a person to leave his or her impoverished life in another country to come and work as domestic help in the United States?

2. What might be some of the red flags that would indicate a worker is not being treated fairly and, in fact, could be a victim of human trafficking?

3. Why is it often not a good idea to ask a person one suspects of being a human trafficking victim if he or she needs help?

4. What kind of fraud can take place to trick a foreign national into moving to the United States, where he or she may become a human trafficking victim?

5. Find a news story featuring a foreign national trafficked into the United States and discuss the story. How might you recognize someone in a similar situation who might need help?

5

An Illusion of Pleasure

Simultaneously, in a culture that takes pride in women's rights and professional achievements, females are commonly portrayed as sexual commodities.

—Demand Report, Shared Hope International[1]

"Consuming pornography is an experience of bought sex. . . . In a very literal way, pornography is advertising for trafficking, not just in general but also in the sense that traffickers and pimps use pornographic images of victims as specific advertising for their 'products,'" says Catherine Mackinon, a professor at Harvard Law School.[2]

She goes on to explain that the addictive hunger porn creates gives way to a drug-like addiction, distorting one's views of sexuality. Viewing porn trains the mind to not only expect sexual gratification on demand, but the addictive nature of this psychological phenomenon drives a person to more escalating content and violent content to create the same high.[3]

One sex buyer (often referred to as a "trick" or "john") interviewed said, "Yes, the woman in pornography is a prostitute. They're prostituting before the cameras. They're getting money from a film company rather than individuals."[4]

Melisa Farley, director of the nonprofit Prostitution Research and Education, says, "When men use pornography, in that process they are trained as tricks. Pornography is men's rehearsal for prostitution. Pornography is cultural propaganda which drives home the notion that women are prostitutes."[5]

A 2007 study interviewed 854 women and men in prostitution in nine countries. Among their findings were that almost half (49 percent) reported that traffickers took pornographic photos of them while they were in prostitution; 47 percent were upset by the buyers' attempts to make them do what they had previously seen in pornography.[6] Additionally, pimps often use porn to "train" their victims in sex acts.

I like to call pornography the gateway drug for purchasing a sex-trafficked individual. Let me be clear though: I am not saying that anyone who views porn will eventually buy a prostitute, nor am I purporting that all porn is straight up human trafficking. But the connection is clear, and porn is a much closer cousin to sex trafficking than it has been perceived in the last few years. I have never heard of a defendant who has been arrested for buying prostitution who has not previously and regularly viewed porn.

The average age when children first encounter pornography is eleven years old.[7] This online sensationalism has fast become the illicit sex education for our young people. "Ninety percent of eight- to sixteen-year-olds in the United States, Canada, Britain, Europe, Japan, and Australia have viewed porn online while doing homework. Eighty percent of fifteen- to seventeen-year-olds have had multiple hard-core exposures. One study of thirteen- and fourteen-year-olds by the University of Alberta found that one-third of boys viewing porn did so 'too many times to count.'"[8]

Many parents have taken precautions to guard their children from viewing pornography. Some have placed their home computer in a common area so others can see what the user is viewing or have installed anti-porn software. Others feel their open relationship with their children results in transparency between them. In reality, 50 percent of teens say they would change their online behavior if they knew their parents were watching.[9]

For the parent who hopes to keep their teen from pornographic websites, it is imperative that they have their child's passwords and regularly monitor accounts. It is also important to let your kids know that you are watching their online usage and will continue to monitor. Additionally, if you find your child has been visiting inappropriate sites, communicate love, acceptance, and forgiveness and not condemnation. A parent who comes alongside to help will have a greater chance of protecting their children than one who lays down rigid rules or shames them. There will be a list of more resources to help your children at the end of this chapter.

It is no wonder we are dealing with a high rate of dating violence in teens. In fact, the violent and sensational nature of porn informs the young and developing mind that sex consists of outlandish and violent acts where body parts, not people, are the basis for sex. Viewing sex as the exploitation of body parts in this manner is a golden path to commercial sex.

Some antislavery proponents believe that sex trafficking is responsible for more slaves than all other types of human trafficking combined. "Sex trafficking is a modern-day form of slavery in which a commercial sex act is induced by force, fraud, or coercion, or in which the person induced to perform such an act is under the age of eighteen years," explains a fact sheet published by the Administration for Children and Families division of the US Department of Health and Human Services.[10] "As defined by the TVPA [Trafficking Victims Protection Act], the term 'commercial sex act' means any sex act on account of which anything of value is given to or received by any person."[11]

Appallingly, the pornography sector of sex trafficking has reached pandemic levels worldwide, with victims forced into various forms of commercial sexual exploitation, including pornography, stripping, live sex shows, prostitution, and mail-order brides.[12] To meet this growing demand, traffickers deceive, coerce, and kidnap unthinkable numbers of women, children, and men, whom they funnel into sex trafficking. Indeed, findings reported in the US House of Representatives' "End Demand for Sex Trafficking Act of 2005" reveal that 100,000 to 300,000 United States children under eighteen are at risk for commercial sexual exploitation every year.[13] And that doesn't take into account the many thousands of young women and men eighteen and over who are trafficked into lives of degradation and pain.

The pornography business preys on these unsuspecting, vulnerable women and youngsters, as well as some young men, in order to satisfy the cravings of their mostly male customers (although females are viewing porn in rapidly increasing numbers).

Although pornography has historically glamorized the idea of being a "porn star," that myth is not reality. Former porn star Shelley Lubben was in the industry in California from 1986 to 1994. She has this to say about it: "The California pornography industry is a destructive, drug infested, abusive, and sexually diseased industry which causes severe negative secondary effects on female and male adult industry workers as well as the general public." Lubben has founded a nonprofit called The Pink Cross, which offers help to those wanting out of the porn industry.[14]

Former porn star Jersey Jaxin describes the horrific experience like this: "You are a number. You're bruised. You have black eyes. . . .

It's not pretty . . . on set. You get hurt. . . . You can say anything you want and they don't listen. They have another scene to go to. It's all about the money. They've forgotten who they are and they don't care who they are hurting."[15]

I have edited her statement to avoid graphic details of the repeated sexual abuse and its resulting injuries. Needless to say, the injuries inflicted in violent porn are real.

Buyers of sexually exploited people try to convince themselves that they're committing a victimless crime—if they even consider it a crime at all—and that willing participants are receiving pleasure. They're wrong on both counts. Many of the people on film are not there voluntarily. And most are treated like slaves, as you will see in the true story about Haley* and her mother, Renee.*[16]

Slaves, Not Models

Haley's voice on the phone was more excited than Renee had ever heard it. "They like me! No more working retail for me, Mom! I'm going to be a model!" Just the tone of Haley's voice made Renee happy for her. Since her graduation from high school two years earlier, Haley had struggled to get money for college tuition and books. She wondered what kind of college classes she could take to prepare her for the modeling career to which she really aspired.

Like all parents, Renee wanted the very best for her daughter. Together they had carefully checked the modeling agency ads, weeding out the ones that looked even the slightest bit shady.

"I go back tomorrow at 2:00 p.m. They want me to sign a contract! They said they have a client who is nationally known and I'm exactly what the client is looking for. Oh Mom, I can't believe this is happening to me! They're going to fly me to Los Angeles right away to begin training, and I'll be making anywhere from five thousand dollars to twenty thousand dollars a month! Are you happy for me?"

Renee *was* happy for her daughter. Even so, she had some concerns. She worried that Haley would become thin and unhealthy. And even though she and Haley had carefully checked out the recognized agency, she realized that there would be no accounting for unscrupulous employees who did not share the upstanding principles the agency advertised.

Still, the last thing she wanted was to squelch Haley's joy. Renee knew that Haley had always wanted to be a star. As early as kindergarten, she had longed for a microphone so she could sing and dance. By her early teens, it was evident to all that Haley was a beauty from head to toe. She had done a couple of small modeling jobs and loved the camera. Even so, she never seemed to be able to get her big break. Now someone had seen the talent and beauty that had been Haley's trademark her whole life. Not only could she finally become all she wanted to be, but she would be paid great money. And that would help more than Renee even wanted to admit.

Renee had raised Haley by herself since her daughter was just four, after Haley's dad left them. With no outside help, financially or otherwise, she and Haley had managed to muddle through, becoming in the process an inseparable team who were as close as mother and daughter could be.

Although for years Renee made good money as a manager in a large software firm, she had lost her job eight months prior due to the recession. To get by, mother and daughter had sold many of their belongings. The house, car, and many of their valuable possessions were gone. In the minimized world with which they had become acquainted, tuition and paying for Haley's college expenses were out of the scope of necessities. So the job offered to Haley appeared to be a godsend.

That night, Renee prepared Haley's favorite chicken cacciatore dinner with extra sauce, and the two laughed and dreamed about how life would be when Haley made it to the big time. Haley tried to describe everyone she'd met at the agency, happily adding that she'd already spotted some gorgeous male models.

As Renee tried to sleep that night, the darkness seemed to bring with it all the worries that can haunt a mother. The next morning as they were bustling around their rented apartment, she asked Haley if it would be okay for her to stop in at the agency. She wanted to meet all the new folks Haley was dealing with for herself.

"Mom! I'm an adult, I'm fine!" Haley exclaimed. "But I would like you to meet everyone; you're going to love them. Why don't you stop in about 4:30? We should be finished with the paperwork by then."

Renee couldn't wait for the end of the day. Everything about the agency had checked out, but this was her baby. Well, not her baby anymore, but her only child. She would die before she would let anything happen to her.

Sometimes Skepticism Isn't Enough

Renee walked in the door of the agency at 4:30 p.m. sharp. The friendly receptionist seemed to be expecting her and, after a warm welcome, brought her to one of the back offices where Haley sat with two staff members. As Renee walked in, the agency employees quickly looked at each other before giving her a warm welcome. "I can see where Haley gets her looks. The fruit didn't fall far from the tree! Which one is the mother and which one is the daughter?" All four laughed. As young looking and gorgeous as Renee was, the question was still ridiculous.

The staff members quickly recapped how excited they were to have found and signed Haley, then began talking to Renee about joining the agency as well. The money they promised after initial training had been completed was unbelievable. Drawing on her financial background, Renee asked some key questions to verify the legitimacy of the offer and the operation. The answers all seemed believable.

A quick photo shoot followed to see how Renee would do in front of the cameras. By 7:00 p.m. both Haley and Renee had been signed. They headed home with tickets in hand and prepared to fly to Los Angeles that weekend. Before departing, they gave away most of the possessions they had left, putting only keepsakes and a few irreplaceable items in storage. Less than a week after Haley's initial meeting at the agency, they boarded the plane, still reeling from their luck. Who knew such financial success could find them so quickly?

At LAX, an attractive man with their names on a small whiteboard met them as they exited the revolving door that led to the baggage area. They soon discovered that he was as amiable as everyone else they had met at the agency.

Upon their arrival at the mansion where they would be living, the caretaker collected their identification and passports in case a trip had to be scheduled while they were on a job. "That's what agents do to help their clients," the caretaker explained. It seemed odd at first not to be carrying any ID. But as the days went on, Renee and Haley found that between makeup, wardrobe, photo shoots, and other appointments, their schedules were packed so full that they didn't seem to need ID or even money, for that matter. The agency paid for all their expenses.

The deal seemed to be getting better and better. The only discordant note was that porn was played much of the time on the house televisions. They were told not to worry. A division of the modeling agency made porn flicks. The divisions, however, were not as separate as initially indicated. Before the week was out, the agency had Haley in nude photo shoots "to build her portfolio and get her comfortable with the cameras." Renee was asked to do some of the risqué photo shoots as well, but because of her age and business experience, they also began training her to recruit other models.

Renee and Haley were disturbed about the porn and uncomfortable with some of the agency requests, but thoughts of their big paychecks at the end of the month made them play along. Payday finally arrived. Mother and daughter opened the envelopes containing their checks with enthusiastic anticipation, only to feel like they'd been blindsided. Neither of them had been paid a dime. Instead, all of their expenses, which the agency had subtracted from their earnings, had been itemized on their pay stubs. Airfare, agent fees, rent, food, transportation, hair, wardrobe, nail salon, makeup and the consultants who told them how to apply it—everything had been bought and paid for on their tab. At the end of the first month, both Haley and Renee owed the company more money than they had earned.

When they approached the caretaker in dismay, she told them that the recruiters had explained all this to them. The fact that such a conversation had never taken place didn't alter the bleak reality that now confronted them. The caretaker then reminded the mother and daughter of the contracts they had signed and told them that they were required by law to at least pay back their debts before they could leave, something they later found out was untrue. "The agency has given you so much," the caretaker concluded. "You haven't even allowed yourselves time to make it big. Why, you're still just learning the business!"

When Renee and Haley expressed concern that the bills were adding up faster than the earnings, the caretaker told them there was a way to make greater money, which could get them out of debt. If Haley was willing to act in more nudes and graduate to sexual actions—and possibly even do some escort dates—the agency would significantly increase her wages and her mom's. Renee flatly refused, but Haley stepped forward anyway. "I'll do it," she said. That evening, Renee was called to an impromptu late-night recruiting session so she would not be able to voice her objections as Haley was led off to her first hard-core porn shoot.

Porn Industry Recruitment

The above story was constructed from the real-life experiences of a midwestern mother and daughter who escaped one day when the mom, who was trusted to recruit, accompanied her daughter on a "modeling job." They are currently still in hiding in the Pacific Northwest because they have heard that the agency that recruited them has put out a contract on their lives.

Here are some of the facts about agency techniques that the two documented after making their escape from the industry:[17]

- Agencies typically drop names of major networks, television shows, and popular men's magazines. It doesn't necessarily mean the agency has any affiliation with anyone associated with those media outlets. It's simply a way to look legitimate to the recruits and draw them in.

- Many young, good-looking men are sent by agencies to college and high school campuses as well as to parties around the country. Their job is to recruit girls in much the same way that pimps recruit victims. Often calling themselves modeling or acting scouts, they use lines like, "Wow, you're so beautiful, you definitely have the looks and body to be a model. I work for a modeling agency in [Miami, New York, Hollywood] and I'd love to submit your photos for some work. I guarantee I can book you solid. I have a couple of companies I work for like [they throw out big names at this point to impress] who are looking for a new model with your exact look. You can make $5,000 to $20,000 a month. We will pay all travel expenses and put you up in a five-star hotel while you're there."

- Some of these young recruiters will also pretend they want to date girls they are trying to recruit. If a girl is skeptical, a recruiter may entice her with a whirlwind courtship. Depending on how much the agency wants the girl, significant money may be spent to recruit her. The recruiters have a budget to impress young women, so they rent upscale hotel rooms and fancy cars to make it look like they are successful. For the girls, the relationship turns into what they think is love. For the recruiters, it remains about the money.

- MySpace, Facebook, Instagram, Snapchat, and other social networks are commonly used to recruit girls. Recruiters work these social networks, which provide them a wealth of information about the potential recruits, including pictures, since many young girls post swimsuit type photos on their profiles. Recruiters wait for a status update that indicates the recruit is emotionally vulnerable (after having had a fight with her mom or boyfriend, for example), then swoop in to offer an attractive alternative.

- Once a girl answers an ad or attends a "casting call," the recruiter convinces her that she's got what it takes to be a star. As soon as the girl believes the hype, the recruiter has her right where he wants her.

- All personal information is gathered, including friends' and family members' names, ages, contact information, financial history, and anything else that may be used at a later date to compel the model to stay and comply with what is asked of her.

111

- Once a new recruit has signed on, she may be given breast implants and other plastic surgery. Agencies don't mention that all the expenses incurred on the model's behalf, including plastic surgery, will have to be paid back to the agency. This isn't revealed until her first paycheck. In typical debt bondage style, once all the expenses have been tallied, she inevitably owes the agency more than she has made and is told she has to continue to work off that debt before she can leave.

- To earn more money, the model is encouraged to do hard-core porn. Once a girl shoots one of the hard-core scenes, she will almost never qualify for the premium roles they said she was perfect for when they recruited her.

- Another path to higher earnings involves servicing private parties. Wealthy and influential guests and even political leaders come to private mansions for what are essentially orgies, where drugs and alcohol are plentiful and serving minors is not restricted. Attendees spend large amounts of cash for films of these parties, which are reserved for private viewing, as well as for the privilege of attending the parties in the first place. Of course, the girls themselves don't usually see any of those proceeds since the money goes directly to the traffickers.

- Once the girl is "modeling," agencies talk about the crossover stars such as Mariah Carey, Sasha Grey, and others who did nude modeling and then became mainstream movie stars. Even if the shoot is in fact hard-core porn, it is always referred to as modeling.

- As soon as a model has done nude photos, the agency will try to shoot a scene involving her sexual interaction with others. After that has been shot and released, the model will be required to view the footage. The vast majority of models hate watching themselves, so this instills shame and encourages the paranoid belief that everyone has now seen them in porn.

- But the profits don't stop there. Once a girl has made it through the indoctrination process, they cut off her photo shoots. The realization that the other girls in the house have photo shoots and she doesn't causes her to doubt herself. At that point, she is encouraged to do "privates," otherwise known as mainstream prostitution. From then on, the agency plays her like a fiddle, alternating between more porn shots to bring up the price for privates and an increasing amount of work in exotic dancing and forced prostitution.

- The more a girl fights for her independence or limits her shoot types, the harder her traffickers will use and abuse her in order to break her spirit. She may be beaten, raped, or used in sadism and masochism (S&M) acts.[18] Don't kid yourself—the beatings and injuries filmed are brutally and disgustingly real, not staged.[19]

The Damage

Pornography in general—and this kind of violent pornography in particular—is on the rise thanks in large measure to the internet. Every year brings the release of 13,000 more porn films that generate $93 billion in annual revenues at the expense of the women and children being sexually exploited on film.[20]

Distribution on the internet has propelled this turn to "gonzo" pornography, a genre that focuses on "body-punishing sex," to use the words of Gail Dines, author of *Pornland*. This horrific on-screen violence is so pronounced that "you've done virtually everything you can to the woman's body short of killing her," says Dines.[21]

I have heard of everything from severe injuries to death as a result of the severe violence that is now commonplace in pornography. This money-driven industry uses real people's lives to cater to the large number of internet users who are viewing porn in record numbers.

Pornography videos hurt more than just those women, men, and even very young children who are forced to participate. Fifty percent of the international sex-trafficking victims in a 2001 survey said that pornography was used to "educate" them into prostitution.[22] In addition, customers will regularly expect the sex-trafficked individuals they frequent to perform the sex acts they have viewed the "actress" on the screen perform.

How will the easy accessibility and increasing frequency of porn in general—and violent porn in particular—influence the sexual behavior of the boys and men who watch it? Only time will tell, but it clearly spreads the message that violence toward women is not only acceptable, it's stimulating.

Money over People

Pornography "legitimizes the buying and selling of women's bodies," says Dines.[23] And that's big business. According to a 2004 ABC News report, there's more money in porn than in the National Football League, National Basketball Association, and Major League Baseball combined.[24] That's understandable when you realize that some of the nation's most recognized corporations profit from bringing porn movies and other productions to the small screen in homes and hotels across the country.

Fighting Fire with Fire

If money is the motivator for the producers of pornography, why not hit them in the wallet? That's part of the rationale behind a recent move toward what is termed a "clean hotel" policy. A company or government entity creates a policy that none of their dollars will be spent for employees to stay in hotels that offer pornography services.

Employees of Winona County, Minnesota, for example, are no longer allowed to stay in hotels that offer pay-per-view pornography. Chuck Derry, cofounder of the Minnesota Men's Action Network, says Minnesota spent $8 billion in 2005 for costs related to sexual violence, three times what the state spent on costs related to drunk driving. In the meantime, Minnesota hotels collected $500 million in revenues off of their pornography offerings.[25]

Voting with our dollars in this way forces free enterprise to change the way business is done. And that moves all of us forward in terms of recognizing—and reclaiming—each other's humanity.

Going the Extra Step—Engage!

Victims of human trafficking, even those being trafficked in pornography businesses, often believe that no one cares about them or their daily suffering. Traffickers and slaveholders are adept at diminishing a person's sense of self-worth and convincing their victims that no one really does care about them. Often victims are told that they are simply being paid for what others are doing for free. That type of talk for the purposes of control and manipulation sets a victim up to stay in the clutches of the trafficker. A victim's subsequent belief that no one will help them is often bolstered by previous deceit and betrayal—sometimes from those closest to them. Consequently, it becomes difficult for victims to trust those who are really trying to help them. Also keep in mind that victims will test anyone trying to help them and will require continued assurance that the ones offering assistance can be trusted and are willing to make the healing trek with them over the long haul.

If you see something that looks like it could be human trafficking, notify local law enforcement or call the National Human Trafficking Hotline at 1-888-373-7888 or text "HELP" to BeFree (233733). This hotline will help you determine if you have encountered victims of human trafficking.

Help for Those with an Appetite for Porn

I would be naïve at best if I didn't acknowledge that of those reading this book, some have struggled with one degree or another of pornography addiction or have known someone who has fought that temptation. As you have seen in this chapter, that struggle affects nearly every one of us on one level or another.

There is some good news in this. You are not alone in the battle, and there is help and hope to believe everyone can be free. Below I have listed some places where you can get help for yourself or loved ones. Many of these resources are drawn from http://porn harmsresearch.com/resources/resources-addicts/, and there you can find even more resources from which to choose.

Research Sources and Help for Pornography Concerns

Compulsion Solutions, http://compulsionsolutions.com

Cure the Craving, http://curethecraving.com

Feed the Right Wolf, http://www.feedtherightwolf.org

Fight the New Drug, http://www.fightthenewdrug.org

International Institute for Trauma and Addiction Professionals, http://www.sexhelp.com

Recovering Couples Anonymous, http://www.recovering-couples .org

Sex Addicts Anonymous, http://saa-recovery.org

Sexaholics Anonymous, http://www.sa.org

Your Brain on Porn, http://yourbrainonporn.com

Religious-Based Recovery Programs

Catholic Support Group for Sexual Addictions Recovery, http://www.saint-mike.org/csgsar

Dirty Girls Ministries, http://dirtygirlsministries.com

Jewish Child and Family Services, http://www.jcfs.org

Muslim Family Services, http://muslimfamilyservices.org/site

Pure Desire Ministries, http://www.puredesire.org

XXX Church, http://www.xxxchurch.com

Filtering and Accountability Software

Covenant Eyes, http://www.covenanteyes.com

Open DNS, http://www.opendns.com/home-internet-security /parental-controls

SpectorSoft, http://www.spectorsoft.com

For Discussion

1. What are some of the places and some of the methods used by producers of pornography to recruit their actors/models/victims?

2. How is debt bondage sometimes used in the production of pornography?

3. Discuss the ripple effect of how pornography harms all those involved in its production, as well as in its consumption.

4. Talk about programs and ways to help someone who is hooked on pornography. How could you encourage someone to get help

without making them feel judged or "less than"? Are there programs near you?

5. Locate a recent news story concerning pornography and discuss how each and every one of us can help in the fight against pornography that is eroding the lives of youth and adults in our communities.

6

What's Love Got to Do with It? Absolutely Nothing!

Today, I stand as a confident woman. I don't carry those negative labels given to me by society anymore. I'm no longer ashamed of my past and I don't blame myself anymore. I had a death sentence over my life from the time I entered into this world. But no matter what trial was put before me, I overcame it.

—Rozlind Saumalu, sex trafficking survivor, leader, and expert

The United States is a place where significant sex trafficking takes place, and a large number of children who are sexually exploited are our own American children. Ernie Allen, in his September 15, 2010, testimony to the US House of Representatives, said of Americans,

Even if they acknowledge that this crime happens in the United States, they assume the victims are foreign children brought into this country who are trafficked only in large cities. In fact, we have learned that most of the victims of domestic minor sex trafficking are American kids who initially leave home voluntarily and are being trafficked on Main Street USA. One police commander said to me, "The only way not to find this problem in any community is simply not to look for it."[1]

The prevalence of sex trafficking, including forced prostitution, is on the rise in part because traffickers have discovered that unlike drugs or weapons, people can be sold over and over again. A criminal who sells illegal drugs or weapons runs a higher risk of arrest and must always be putting out more cash to replenish their supply. In selling a human being, a trafficker brutally sells the person over and over. I have heard gang members declare that it's a better business to sell "hoes" than drugs. If a police car pulls over a gang member, good luck explaining two kilos of cocaine taped under the dashboard. But if he just has his "nieces" in the car and is "heading to my uncle's house," law enforcement has little recourse when the girls and others back up his fictitious story. Once the two keys of coke is gone, dealers have to get more; human beings can be sold over and over again with very little risk. The bottom line in human trafficking is always money in exchange for people's lives, which is why I consider it perhaps the most torturous crime on the planet.

"Human traffickers profit by turning dreams into nightmares," says Michael Garcia, a US attorney in Manhattan. "These women sought a better life . . . and found instead, forced prostitution and misery."[2] Sadly, the same can be said about thousands of children as well.

A Life Lost

For most of us and for most of our children, turning thirteen and finally becoming a teenager is a time of excitement and anticipation.

At that age, I hoped my parents would let me walk to the store alone or go to a movie or a roller-skating party with my friends without adult supervision. My most grown-up "naughtiness" at thirteen involved sneaking a little eye shadow, passing carefully folded notes to my girlfriends in class, or muttering a swear word when no adult was listening.

For thirteen-year-old Tiffany Mason,[3] life looked much different. She and her twin brother William had been born to Lori Torres in San Francisco, California, in 1986. The eighties were an era when people in the "me generation" seemed to live for self-fulfillment and happiness "for today." Sometimes that resulted in a mentality where people didn't think ten minutes past what was right in front of their noses. As a part of that culture, and as a result of her difficult life, Lori listened more to the drug-addicted monster inside of her than the voice telling her to be a good mother.

By February 1988, Lori's lifestyle and drug addiction had caught up with the young mother. Tiffany and William were sent off to live with family in California and Washington State, and were then juggled from relative to relative for the next eleven years. Consistency and roots would never be a part of their childhood. Although Tiffany craved loving, consistent discipline from someone, it was rarely available to her. She once told her cousin Jody Jensen, "I like coming to your house, because you have rules here."[4]

Despite the hard hand she'd been dealt, Tiffany remained positive, always believing life would somehow get better. Meanwhile, the twins' mother, Lori, continued to live a fast and irresponsible lifestyle until the late nineties when she began sobering up. Finally, in 1999, Tiffany and William were allowed to return to live with the mother they had only been able to visit sporadically. By then Lori had remarried and given birth to two additional children. So Tiffany and William shared their new home—room 305, a cramped and cluttered old room in the West Hotel on Eddy Street in the

Tenderloin district of San Francisco—with their mother, her new husband, and two toddlers.[5]

The seedy hotel room was no place to reunite with and raise thirteen-year-old twins, and not just because of the lack of space. The Tenderloin district is infamous for its drug addicts, dealers, and prostitution (and combinations thereof). It's not unusual to see people passed out in a doorway, lying in their own urine. It is also known as one of the roughest and most dangerous places for sex-trafficked individuals to walk the "track" (slang for the area where those selling sex solicit customers). Anything goes in the Tenderloin district.

Young Target

Tiffany had just outgrown the stage in which many young girls play with dolls and imagine what adult life will be like while playing house. As the friendly youngster who loved to giggle and laugh began to venture out of her hotel room home onto Eddy Street, however, those childhood memories would soon be far behind her. At four-foot-eleven, a shapely young woman's figure was already beginning to emerge from her preadolescent, more rounded body, and her pretty hazel eyes and wide, bright, innocent smile were endearing. Tragically, a thirteen-year-old virgin is like a neon money sign to the pimps who frequent that area looking for vulnerable girls to sell, especially since young girls bring more money than older girls because of their innocent and tender ways.[6]

Before long, Tiffany began coming home with hundred-dollar bills. When questioned, she confessed to her mom that the money belonged to Damien "Pairadice" Posey, the pimp who allegedly trafficked Tiffany.[7]

Stories of young girls being recruited by pimps into forced prostitution are not as uncommon as one might hope. Twelve to fourteen is the average age that a girl is first turned out for commercial sexual exploitation.[8]

Lori Torres, who worked at Blondies Pizza trying to support her family, could all too readily imagine the danger and trouble ahead for her daughter Tiffany if she continued to live in the Tenderloin district. So although she was glad to finally have her children back despite the inevitable stress involved, she immediately relocated the family to Santa Rosa where she had relatives. Lori and her young family took up residence in a Motel 6, and she found a job waiting tables at the Hungry Hog Restaurant. When DHS learned that Lori had moved to a hotel out of the county, however, they brought the twins back to foster care, placing Tiffany in a group home only ten to fifteen minutes away from the Tenderloin district.

The ninth grader immediately started staying out late, worrying her foster mother. Then Tiffany began bringing home "gifts" typically given to victims by their pimps, such as stiletto shoes and seductive clothing. In Tiffany's case, those gifts were also accompanied by fresh bruises. Back under the pimp control of Pairadice, after just three weeks she threw all her belongings in plastic bags and left in his glossy black Ford Explorer. It should have been no surprise to DHS, or to anyone else who understands the dynamics of a girl who has been trafficked, that Tiffany would reconnect with her pimp and quit school or that he would once again traffic her.

Hindered by the Social Services Designed to Help

Tiffany's mom went to battle for her daughter. She reported what she knew about Pairadice, hoping to prompt his arrest and Tiffany's subsequent release from his grasp.[9] When the authorities did nothing, Lori's hands were tied. "I was homeless, not on drugs. They took away my parental rights and then didn't take responsibility for my kids," says Lori.[10] "I wasn't a good mother. But if you're going to take my kids, then protect them."[11]

A few months later, Pairadice was arrested and Tiffany chose to move back with her mother illegally rather than stay in a group home. But that didn't last long. The twisted, addictive lure of "the life" is strong once a girl has been seasoned and turned out as a sex slave. It is nigh to impossible to explain that unreasonable and insatiable pull, but Tiffany continued to go back, as the majority of girls do. When she was picked up by law enforcement for prostitution, the authorities insisted she be put back in the group home even though they should have suspected she wouldn't stay.

"The [social services] system sets up a girl to go AWOL," Laurel Freeman, a counselor at the Youth Guidance Center, told *Examiner* staff reporter Adrienne Sanders, author of a five-part series titled "Poster Child for Broken Promises." "[The girl] has suffered trauma on the streets. She has a pimp hanging over her. It's easier for them to stick her in a group home—even when they know she's going to run—than it is to come up with something different. It's like a tar pit, miring the girls farther down."[12]

Pairadice knew exactly what to do to maintain his hold on Tiffany. Although she wanted to go back to school, he kept pimping her. He even picked her up in front of Francisco Middle School and later Mission High School, as well as two group homes and the DHS shelter.[13] It was as if the system allowed pimps like Pairadice the same access as a responsible family member.

He also kept Tiffany away from people who would try to help her break free from the life, and he even threatened to kill one shop owner who tried to help her by occasionally buying her a meal or allowing her to sleep on his couch.[14]

Pairadice let Tiffany know who was boss. He pulled her hair often—one time even dragging her down the street by her hair. He strangled her. A second pimp called Bautiese "B. Rich" Richardson, a self-proclaimed "super pimp" well known for pimping young girls like Tiffany, pimped her as well. Amazingly, both men had worked in city youth programs as mentors. B. Rich was also known for his violence against the girls he pimped. After beatings he would tell the girls, "I'm sorry, you know I don't like to hit you." They were made to feel like it was their fault that B. Rich "had" to hit them.[15]

It is not known how, why, or exactly when Tiffany was shifted back and forth between the pimps like the trump card in a game, but it is a well-known fact that between them they controlled Tiffany's every move. Pimps decide, among other things, where a girl will go, whom she will see, and what she will wear. In Tiffany's case, Pairadice decided that her hair would be bleached blonde. "We'll make more scratch [money] that way, Little Momma," he told her. "Dudes dig blondes and you know it."[16]

The life Tiffany lived, as a child whose body was sold multiple times a night to strangers on the streets, was no secret to anyone. Her mother knew and could do nothing to help. Her brother, who was mired in a boys' foster home where it was reported that the counselors smoked blunts (marijuana-filled cigars) and drank brandy with him and the other foster boys, could do nothing to help.[17] The police knew and would pick her up for prostitution, take her mace and money, and drop her off at the DHS shelter where she was unable to receive the help she needed.

Once, when one of her "regular" customers, a forty-nine-year-old man, was caught having sex with Tiffany, he was cited on a misdemeanor of soliciting a prostitute instead of for statutory rape or child molestation.[18] According to the Trafficking Victims Protection Act (TVPA), any person under eighteen years old engaging in a commercial sex act (that is, exchanging a sex act for something of value) is a victim of severe human trafficking. According to that definition, there is no such thing as a "child prostitute." Citing a sex buyer for soliciting a prostitute instead of arresting him for buying sex with a child only reinforced what Tiffany had been told repeatedly by her traffickers and others—that she was a "prostitute" and that's all she was good for.

Nobody Should Be a Throwaway

"Protecting johns like this is collusion," said the late Norma Hotaling, founder of the First Offenders Prostitution Program. "And it gave Tiffany the message that she was a 'toss-away.'"[19] Surprisingly, neither the streets nor the message of worthlessness hardened Tiffany. "Keep your head up," she always told her friends.[20]

Despite her own difficult circumstances, Tiffany, who loved children, especially those with disabilities, still cared about others and did what she could to help them. "Tiffany was a bright spot in my life and she was generous," says her cousin Jody Jensen. During a time when Jensen and her family were surviving on macaroni and cheese, Tiffany came and filled their refrigerator with groceries. Jensen told Tiffany, "I know where you get your money. You don't have to do that, you're a fourteen-year-old little girl." Tiffany helped them out anyway.[21]

Sometimes when I've told her story, people have questioned why Tiffany, as a sex-trafficked girl, occasionally had money to spend or give away. While we know that pimps demand 100 percent of the girls' money, some victims have been known to risk stashing small amounts of cash for a prospective escape or to help a family member as Tiffany did. Tiffany, however, would never get the assistance *she* so obviously needed.

One person, veteran child welfare social worker John Paul Carobus, did his best to help Tiffany, whom he called a "wounded dove."[22] Although he saw what was needed and tried to give her the services she deserved, he met with repeated opposition from his superiors. DHS bureaucrats seemed to be more interested in protecting their own reputations and preventing legal liabilities against themselves and their department than in saving Tiffany's life.

Even so, Carobus made repeated attempts to get Tiffany off the streets. One afternoon he saw her sitting in an outdoor café on Market Street and ran across the street to greet the person he termed "the delightful brat."[23] He bought her lunch and talked to her about leaving the area to go be with some of her family in Santa Rosa, where her great-grandmother was celebrating a big birthday. Tiffany initially rejected his advice, but the thought of visiting certain relatives softened her resistance. After expressing embarrassment at her relatives seeing her in what she called "ho clothes," she allowed Carobus to buy her a new outfit at Marshalls that would be more appropriate and to put her on a bus to her relatives.[24]

Knowing her lifestyle and that she was likely to go missing, Carobus asked a passerby to snap a picture of the two of them before she left. He figured with that picture, he could at least have something to put on a missing-child poster when it was needed. One might think that the higher-ups at DHS would applaud such caring actions toward a child so desperately in need of attention. Instead, Carobus was berated in front of his co-workers at a subsequent staff meeting. "I'm giving you a direct order," Carobus's superior told him. "If you see her again you don't go talk to her. . . . You could be liable."[25] When Tiffany eventually did go missing, Carobus requested permission to print the picture he had taken for a poster to be distributed in the search for her. His request was denied by the city attorney's office.[26]

Tiffany did not remain in Santa Rosa long. When Lori Torres went looking for Tiffany in San Francisco on June 5, 2001, she knew her daughter was in trouble and must have wanted to help her in the worst way. She found Tiffany on Mission Street and took her to KFC, where they ate dinner together.[27]

Tiffany knew she was in danger, as well as who was responsible. A few months earlier she had told Lori, "If anything happens to me, Mom, make [Pairadice] pay."[28]

Tiffany and her mother discussed Tiffany's current situation as they ate their chicken and mashed potatoes. Finally, Tiffany relented. "I'll go with you," she told her mother. "But I need some cash first. I'll be back in a half hour."

Without any legal rights to detain her own daughter, Torres couldn't stop Tiffany from getting into a shiny black Lexus and leaving. She waited in vain for her return. Torres would never see her daughter alive again.[29]

On July 31, police picked up Tiffany at 18th and Capp Streets. When their computer check revealed that Tiffany was a missing juvenile, officers dropped her at a DHS shelter. Tiffany called her mom and begged her to come and pick her up. Although she had spent nearly two years in the dangerous and degrading life of being forced into prostitution by adult pimps, she was still too young to drive. But Torres had no gas and no money. She told her daughter to ask the staff at DHS to put her on a bus home to her mother. Later that night, Sprint shut off Lori Torres's cell phone for non-payment. That was the last conversation she and her daughter would ever have.[30]

The Circuit

Lori would find out after Tiffany's death that on August 3, four days after their last conversation, Pairadice had driven Tiffany to Sacramento. Pimps often move their victims from city to city, and even from state to state, to minimize the chances of victims successfully reaching out for help and to satisfy the wants of those who buy sex from children like Tiffany. In the process, they increase their profits by providing variety for the sex buyers in the alternating venues, and the movement also helps them escape detection by law enforcement agents.[31] After a couple of weeks, pimps again relocate their victims to the next place. "The bottom line is that they keep moving, especially [when] a child is [involved]," says Keith Bickford, a US Marshal working against human trafficking in the state of Oregon. "If a kid leaves foster care and ends up with a pimp, that kid is gone . . . within a couple hours. We've found them down in Las Vegas and we've found them up in Seattle."[32] Along the way, truck stops and strip clubs serve to season newly turned-out victims and provide plenty of clients to pad the money clips of pimps.

The objective is to keep the trafficked individual producing income, no matter what. If she looks like she's on the verge of getting help, she's moved. And if she gets pregnant, that's taken care of too. Forced abortions are not uncommon among sex-trafficked girls. It makes no difference to the pimp if she wants to keep her child. One Mexican girl who had been trafficked across the border complained about terrible vaginal pain to no avail. "I asked repeatedly to be taken to the doctor. No one ever took me," she recalled. "But they did take the girls who became pregnant to a doctor where they performed forced abortions."[33]

The sex slave's health and well-being is simply not an issue. Neither is her safety, as Tiffany's story shows in heartbreaking detail. Tiffany was killed on August 4, the day after being driven to Sacramento. Her pimp, Pairadice, states that he remembers seeing her cross Stockton Boulevard and get into the car of a man who paid to have sex with her.

Five days later, a fisherman reported catching sight of a corpse drifting slowly with the current in Lake Natoma. Folsom police cast a large net and dragged out Tiffany's nude body. Local campers, park rangers, law enforcement personnel, and medical examiners stood and watched the operation from the shoreline. Security officers stood guard on the edge of the crime tape to keep the public and reporters at bay.[34]

John Carobus, the social worker who had tried on many occasions to help Tiffany, had been denied permission to print her picture on the missing child poster because California law states that the child's confidentiality can't be broken. "Tiffany's confidentiality certainly was broken when she was floating in the lake," he remarked bitterly when her body was found.[35]

It is not known how many sex-trafficked children like Tiffany are murdered by sex buyers or by their pimps. They're usually estranged from their families, so their relatives might not even know they are missing and be able to report it.

"They're not going to file a missing person's report," a former pimp told me in an interview. "Her family may assume, 'Oh, she's probably out doing something bad somewhere and nobody really knows where she is.'"[36] Pimps won't report a girl missing—or even check with the family to see if she has run home—because the finger will be pointed toward them. Besides, according to pimps, the girls are expendable. "There's a big window of opportunity for girls to become [murder] victims [without anyone knowing]," the pimp told me. "It could be months to years before they're ever found." If they're found at all.

Pimps Recruiting on the Internet

Tiffany was trafficked from 1999 to 2001, when most sex was still solicited on the streets and most victims were recruited in person. A growing demand for purchasing sex has now made the internet the most prominent place that victims are sex-trafficked. Traffickers still recruit in person but also utilize the internet and gaming sites to recruit behind the guise of a computer where they can easily assume varied identities.

Traffickers often troll for young teens in chat rooms and even younger children playing online video games. Xbox and PlayStation have become an avenue for complete strangers to communicate with our children while they are distracted with games. Sometimes they let the potential victim win in an attempt to establish a relationship. In many video games, playing with strangers in your own living room is the norm or even required for the game. Predators use these games to tell unsuspecting children whatever they need to in order to suck them into their web. Online threats such as these have substantially broadened the numbers of children now at risk. Before the easy access into our homes via the internet, perpetrators "had to sell the dream face-to-face . . . one girl at a time," said Dallas police sergeant Byron Fassett, of the high-risk victim and trafficking unit. "Now the pond to fish out of just got even bigger."[37]

After befriending a young person online for days, weeks, or even months, the trafficker often talks the youngster into running away from home to meet them. Once they are out of the protection of their home, the trafficker has great latitude to continue the process of grooming and begin trafficking the youngster for profit.

Selling Flesh Online

Using the internet to recruit victims as well as to connect sex buyers with sex—a huge and fast-growing method for the "marketing" of victims—provides consumers of sex with anonymity as well as relatively easy access to nearly anything sexual that could be desired. "The Internet serves as a virtual clearinghouse, a sex bazaar connecting demand and supply," wrote one observer.[38]

The underhanded use of the internet to connect buyers of human flesh with those being sold isn't limited to online porn sites or other sexually-oriented webpages. Shockingly, traffickers and others who sexually exploit unsuspecting victims frequent many well-known websites with legitimate uses—sites such as Facebook, Instagram, MySpace, and Snapchat.

Craigslist, which was the first well-known site to have an adult services section, has discontinued their adult services ads within the United States (although law enforcement occasionally still recovers trafficking victims as a result of investigating some Craigslist ads). The *New York Times* estimates that those discontinued ads would have brought in $44 million to Craigslist in 2010, the year they shut down.[39] While Craigslist succumbing to public pressure is good news, this is a drop in the bucket. Children and adults continue to be marketed online as sexual commodities. Still, it does prove that we as the public have the power to pressure businesses into cleaning up their acts.

In addition to connecting buyers to sex-trafficked individuals, the internet also facilitates the trafficking of women from foreign countries into the United States through "marriage" to American men who use online mail-order bride services. Most mail-order brides coming to America have little understanding of their basic rights, and too often they are abused, sexually exploited, or recruited into forced prostitution almost as soon as they set foot on American soil. "I didn't plan to go in for prostitution," said one such woman. "I just wanted to be a wife."[40]

Sex Tourism

Sex tourism, defined as traveling to a foreign country with the intent to engage in sexual activity with a child, has become another unfortunate part of American human trafficking. It is illegal for a US citizen to engage in such activity, which is prosecutable under the Trafficking Victims Protection Act. The fact that it's illegal does not stop it from happening. American sex tourism is prevalent in a number of countries, including Cambodia, where Americans make up 38 percent of that country's sex tourists, and in Costa Rica, where Americans make up 80 percent of their sex tourism visitors.[41] Overall, it is estimated that Americans make up about 25 percent of all sex tourists around the world.[42]

Sex buyers often attempt to justify their actions by saying they are giving money to children who are being sold for sex so the children and their families can eat, or that sex is not looked upon the same way in many foreign cultures. Both of those arguments are absolutely empty. Sex tourism is a form of human trafficking. Like any other form of human trafficking, the trafficker is the one ultimately profiting, not the victims or their families. Also, we must never downplay the fact that paid sex disregards the humanity of the victim and is horrifically damaging to a person of any culture. If the buyers' intent was to benefit children in foreign countries, they could instead give their money to any of a multitude of humanitarian agencies instead of spending their money to exploit innocent victims.

Warning: It *Can* Happen to Your Kids

Americans, however, certainly don't have to travel outside our borders to buy sex. Even sex with a child or young adult is readily available right in our communities. American-born US citizens, our daughters and sons, make up the largest portion of sex-trafficked minors in the United States.[43] Though statistics aren't clear regarding the number of children like Tiffany and Sarah, whom you met earlier in this book, we do know that the average age range of a child first forced into prostitution is twelve to fourteen for girls and eleven to thirteen for boys, with some much, much younger.

It is difficult for most people, especially those who grew up in fairly "normal" families, to understand that teenage girls from families like yours and mine regularly fall for the tactics pimps use. "When they hear the term 'child trafficking,' most Americans naïvely believe that it only happens somewhere else, in Southeast Asia or Central America," reads Ernie Allen's written testimony presented to the US House of Representatives.[44]

Unfortunately, some in our country appear determined to believe just that. One day I talked to an educator who knew a significant amount about international trafficking but seemed to take the position that human trafficking wasn't a problem in middle-class America.[45] He struck me as someone who considered human trafficking to be a political problem more than a national and international crisis that affects real people—even our own daughters, sisters, sons, and brothers. I also realized that this man didn't understand just how widespread and pervasive the danger of human trafficking really is in the United States. So I asked him, "What if one of your daughters, when she becomes a teenager, is lured into being friends with an online predator—on Facebook, MySpace, Instagram, or Xbox Live—and that predator talks her into meeting him, and she becomes a victim?"

His answer reaffirmed my belief that one of the biggest obstacles to stopping human trafficking in the United States is that people don't believe it can happen to them or to their loved ones. "She's not vulnerable, because we don't live in poverty," he answered. "It's not possible, because we are middle class, not poor. This is about poverty."[46]

This kind of thinking concerns me. While it's true that traffickers and pimps prey much more often on the underprivileged and economically vulnerable than on those in the middle classes and above, the simple truth is that under certain circumstances, anyone, regardless of their economic and social status, can fall into the hands of traffickers and pimps. We saw that in the story about Sarah in chapter 1 of this book.

Unfortunately, in the majority of stories I hear, the victim and their family didn't believe sex trafficking could happen to them. Human trafficking can happen to any child.

The notion that this is about only impoverished, abused, at-risk children simply is not true and is one of the myths that has hindered the level of awareness about human trafficking. This is the second-largest and fastest-growing crime in the world. Yet in our middle and high schools we have mandatory curriculum about drugs and bullying, but seldom hear any talk about human trafficking.

Until we can raise awareness to the point that we all—normal citizens, civic leaders, government officials, law enforcement, social services, and others—know it can happen to anyone, we will not win this battle.

It can and it does happen to anyone. One only needs to ask my friend Kayla.[47*] Her mother was a real estate agent and her father was a police captain. She had obviously been warned repeatedly about stranger danger and other such pitfalls. However, at seventeen years old she was unsuspecting when a seemingly gentle and caring man befriended her as she worked the cosmetic counter at a high-end department store.

I recently asked Kayla if her parents had ever warned her about trafficking and that it could happen to her. "It's an unspoken issue in a lot of families because they don't think it could happen to them, or don't even know about the issue, or are too scared to even acknowledge anyone they love could be a potential target." Like many traffickers, the man targeting Kayla watched her for days before he approached her. She had no idea she was being watched, but by the time he first talked to her, he knew her daily habits, how she interacted with people, her food and clothing preferences, and what kinds of topics would interest her. "I guess my pimp got lucky when he started watching me."

For Kayla, the seemingly kind and gentle man turned out to be a brutal pimp who trafficked her for almost three years. During that time he regularly took her phone and sent disrespectful texts to her parents and other family members, lying to them and telling them Kayla didn't want them in her "business."

As a result, her family had no idea she was being trafficked and instead thought she had made bad choices about friends, drugs, college, and jobs. They called her the "black sheep" of the family, which further reinforced the message she was constantly receiving from her trafficker.

Preying on the Weak

Pimps and traffickers know how to sniff out and exploit vulnerability, and not just the kind that comes from living in situations of poverty, neglect, and abuse. The most prevalent common denominator for trafficking victims is a history of sexual abuse. According to one study, 70 to 85 percent of sex workers report childhood sexual abuse.[48] This is why when I am speaking to a group of young people, I often address the topic of sexual abuse and urge them to tell a responsible adult if they have been sexually abused and to get counseling to facilitate their healing from that trauma.

Perpetrators know that in many cases just being a typical teenager can make any young girl vulnerable. As the mother of two adult children, I understand how even teenagers who grow up in solid homes go through times of insecurity, times when they want to experience new things and push against the boundaries and limitations their parents place on them. In addition, even the most well-balanced, emotionally happy teen living in a loving, affirming home can go through seasons when she believes (often wrongly) that she is not loved or appreciated at home or liked at school. These normal insecure feelings and emotional stages in the lives of healthy, normal teens make them vulnerable to human trafficking predators.

Yes, pimps are predators. The very nature of the word *predator* should give us a good idea of how pimps operate. Every spring in central Oregon, people begin to venture into the woods to hike, camp, and fish. During that time of year, local television channels broadcast news spots to instruct the public about what to do if they encounter a cougar in the woods with cautions like: "Anyone spotting a cougar should take certain steps—don't run, but make a noise and appear as large as possible. Open your coat if you have one. Raise your arms, but do not turn your back. If attacked, fight back and use whatever might be available. Always keep children and pets close by when hiking in cougar habitat."

Cougars, like most predatory wild animals, can spot vulnerability. If the cougar sees a small human, a child, or a small animal, it is likely to attack because it knows it can win the fight. An adult who curls up in a ball upon coming into visual contact with a cougar is likely to be attacked because the animal perceives the human has become small and defenseless.

The same principle holds true with predators who are traffickers and pimps. They aren't guided by any sense of morality or of right and wrong, only by the feeling that they can overpower certain targets. Of course, when it comes to young children, their intentions of victimizing a young person become easier because of the naïve nature of their potential victim. Like a cougar stalking a child, they swoop in for the kill.

Easy Pickings

Until now, we have talked mainly about American girls becoming victims of sex trafficking. However, girls who are foreign nationals are sometimes trafficked into our country, and even boys, both foreign nationals and US citizens, can be victims of sex trafficking.

Arturo*⁴⁹ did what he always did when he was nervous or bored or afraid. As the van bounced along the rough Mexican road, he ran his brown calloused fingers over the rosary that belonged to his mother. He was excited and nervous to be going with Marco,* a twenty-something Mexican American who had offered him a new life and a job in America. Not only was the salary good, but his duties would include being an extra in the movies. Once when he was twelve, Arturo had gone to see a movie with his friends. He had heard of movie stars and the life of luxury they lived, and he dreamed of having his own house, plenty of food, and even a shiny black sports car with flashy chrome wheels.

When his mother was alive, they had taken care of one another. She would often sing to him as he was going to sleep at night, and he would think of funny jokes to make her smile. He had never known his father, and he had grown up feeling like the man of the house. He knew how to work hard and also how to raise everyone's spirits.

He had loved to see his mother's smile, so it bothered him that now, just a few months after her death, he sometimes had trouble remembering her face. He promised her he would never forget her and would make her proud.

Since his mother's death, Arturo had taken odd jobs handing out flyers for a promotional company to earn enough money for food. He had been hired partially because of his good looks and charm, which seemed to be an asset that opened doors for him. But now he had the opportunity to live up to his deathbed promise. He rubbed the beads of the rosary between his fingers and thought of how proud she would be of him going to America all by himself at only fourteen years of age.

Arturo slept through the night in the van traveling to America, his stomach no longer aching with hunger because Marco had fed him tortillas as well as potato chips and cookies. As daylight broke and they neared the Tijuana border, Arturo wondered if they would really let him cross. He had heard stories of others who had paid large sums to come to America and had been turned away at the border. Marco told him that after he arrived, he would only have to pay back his transportation costs with his earnings, which wouldn't take long with the great job he was about to get.

At the border station, a man with a gruff voice asked Marco for their papers, which Marco quickly produced. Soon they were speeding along the freeway on the American side of the border. Arturo gazed out in absolute amazement at the Southern California homes they passed. Riches seemed to be everywhere. He was going to have a better life than he had even dreamed.

When they got to Oceanside, Marco took him to a house with boarded-up windows in a neighborhood much nicer than the ones he had known in Mexico, though not as nice as the houses they had passed along the way. As they walked inside the front door with its four dead bolts, Marco spoke with a man named Tito.* After an argument about price, Marco accepted some money from Tito and left Arturo with him.

There were two other boys and also two girls living in the house, all four about Arturo's age. He was happy to meet other kids, but they seemed to be very guarded in all their actions and spoke very few words. One boy, Martin,* seemed friendlier than the others, almost as if he wanted a friend as much as Arturo did. They exchanged names and nervous glances.

Nighttime came and the children were all allowed a small portion of beans and rice from the big meal they had prepared for the adults who lived there. It wouldn't be long before Arturo found out why the children seemed so afraid.

Just after dark, Tito began opening the door to various men. Arturo was told to sit on the couch with the other children as the men looked them over. The first man took one of the girls into another room. A few minutes later Martin was told to go with a man into the next room.

As Martin shuffled off with the man, another unshaven American man with gray in his red-colored beard and hair pointed to Arturo. He was told to stand up and turn in a circle so the man could see him front and back. When the man nodded his head, Arturo was told to go to the back bedroom with him.

What happened in that room could only be described as worse than Arturo's worst nightmare. Arturo fought the man's advances to no avail. After the forced sex, Arturo scrambled to get his clothes back on and curled up in a fetal position on the bed. Tito came in within a few minutes and hit him across the face with his fist. "Quit being a baby and get out on the couch," he demanded. There were more customers to serve. The small amount of rice and beans came up Arturo's throat as he took a quick detour to the bathroom.

Arturo serviced three other customers that night. His body screamed in pain by the time he fell asleep just before dawn. He had heard of places like this but never dreamed he would be trapped in such a hellhole. And trapped he was. With the windows boarded and the doors locked, he barely saw daylight. He understood now that there was no promotional job, no acting as a movie extra. Instead, he had been brought here to "work" in this brothel.

Martin seemed to understand what Arturo was feeling and offered an occasional understanding smile. He even helped Arturo with his daytime chores of scrubbing the baseboards and floors. As the months went on, the two boys developed as much of a friendship as was allowed. Although Arturo would never get used to the men using him for sex every night, the friendship with Martin helped him cope.

During that time, however, Tito became more and more violent. He had frequently threatened Arturo with his big knife. One Thursday evening, he actually used it. While cooking the evening meal for Tito and his friends, Arturo had accidentally burned some of the potatoes. Tito was furious. In the beating that ensued, he cut Arturo's thigh almost to the bone. The wound bled so much that Tito realized it was going to need medical attention. He called a friend who was a nurse to sew up the wound. As the gentle man carefully stitched and dressed the wound, Arturo thought this might be a way out. But his hopes were soon dashed when he was required to give the nurse "payment" for this medical service. It seemed that no one would help him, and the severe pain in his leg matched the hopelessness in his heart.

As the months wore on, he and Martin dreamed together of a time they could live in the "America, Land of the Free" they had been promised. They wondered aloud how long they could endure being enslaved in this prison and the nightly shame and pain. Martin had been there longer than Arturo and had started younger. It seemed like their incarceration and sexual exploitation was harder on him than on any of the other kids. Despite the comfort he took in Arturo's friendship, Martin began to withdraw. Arturo knew the life was getting the better of his closest friend.

It had been a particularly rough week for all the kids. In addition to increasing numbers of customers, Tito was drinking more and more. At 4:00 a.m., the customers finally quit coming for the night. Arturo noticed that his friend Martin had been in the bathroom for some time and decided to check on him.

He opened the door a crack, then saw blood covering the floor and splattered all over the sink, cabinet, tub, and toilet. As fear gripped him, he pushed open the door. Martin lay in a pool of his own blood, without breath, without pulse. As Arturo screamed his friend's name over and over again, the other children came rushing in, followed by Tito.

Tito picked up Martin's body, roughly shoving it under one arm. As Martin's hair flicked blood on the carpet and walls, Tito lugged his limp body down the hallway and gruffly barked orders to the other children to clean up the mess. "I'd better not be able to see one drop of Martin's filthy blood when I return," he ordered.

The next two years were harder for Arturo. He had lost his only friend in the world and had learned in the process not to allow himself to get close to—or to feel for—the others. He kept to himself and survived by pretending he was someone else, somewhere else when the men came to use him each night. Sometimes he wondered whether he should end it all as Martin had done. The memory of Martin's blood always stopped him from following through.

One particularly hot and humid day, after Tito and his cohorts had consumed plenty of drugs and liquor while celebrating a birthday, Tito opened one of the high windows in the kitchen so that a fresh breeze would blow through the house. He then continued to party. Eventually, the men passed out and the children saw their first chance to escape. Arturo and Victor,* the boy who had replaced Martin, wriggled through the open window. They tried to pull the two girls through the opening but couldn't manage to get them out. When Tito awoke and began to yell, the two boys ran.

Arturo and Victor had no idea where they were going but knew they never wanted to go back to that house. So they forced themselves to keep running even when they felt they could go no farther. They were convinced that if Tito found them, they would be killed. On the outskirts of Oceanside, they found a park where many homeless persons and illegal aliens gathered. There Arturo was befriended by a couple. Eventually he came to trust them and told them about his horrific ordeal of coming to America.

The caring couple sought out options for Arturo and found a place for him across the country in Florida. There he received shelter, counseling, education, and acceptance. His caseworker cared for him in genuine ways and believed in him. Although his trauma was great, little by little the healing began.

Arturo is now in his twenties and is finishing school to become a social worker. After experiencing the support he needed, he wants to help others who may have experienced hard lives to overcome their issues the way he has.

He carries regret that will last a lifetime about having to leave the girls at the brothel that night. Because he couldn't provide the police with the location of the house once he finally learned to trust the authorities, nothing was ever done about the operation, and to his knowledge the other kids were never rescued.

How might one recognize a house where children or adults are sex trafficked in our neighborhoods? Some red flags might be cars coming and going at all hours of the day and night, children or adults who can sometimes be seen through the windows but are rarely outside, children who do not leave for school each day, or sounds of violence such as screaming or banging. If you see some of these signs in a home in your neighborhood, you can call local law enforcement or the National Human Trafficking Hotline 1-888-373-7888 or text "HELP" to BeFree (233733).

Protecting Children from Sex Traffickers

As a parent myself, I know the fear and terror that can strike the heart of a parent reading these accounts. You may be asking yourself

143

what you can do to protect your children from becoming a victim
of sex trafficking. I have listed some suggestions below:

- Educate your kids about human trafficking: that it exists,
  what it looks like, and to talk to you or another responsible adult if they think they see it. If they are emotionally
  ready, have them read this book to help them recognize the
  red flags.

- Communicate with your kids and let them talk to you without
  judgment. They need to know they are safer with you than
  anywhere else. One rule we had with our kids was that if they
  did something wrong and they told us before we found out,
  they might have some consequences, but their punishment
  would be less than if we found out another way.

- Technology is a big part of how sex trafficking happens
  with kids. Know your kids' passwords and what is on their
  phones. A good rule is to say, "As long as you live under
  our roof, we have access to passwords, emails, texts, etc."
  Your child's privacy is important, but so is their safety. If
  you talk to parents whose children have been sex trafficked,
  without exception they will all tell you they wish they had
  done that. Also, GPS tracking devices on phones can be
  key to tracking your child and finding them when they first
  go missing.

- Know your kids' friends. Have them over to your home. Feed
  them a pan of brownies or a batch of cookies, and sit down
  and talk with them. Know where they hang out and what
  they are like.

- Get your kids involved in positive things: community youth
  groups, sports, music, community service, and church youth
  groups. Surround them with positive peer pressure.

For Discussion

1. The material in this chapter is possibly the most disturbing in this book. Feeling sad and disturbed about the material is a normal reaction. If you are reading this book as a group study, discuss your feelings with your group. If you are reading this book alone, find a friend or relative with whom you can discuss your feelings.

2. Prostitution has often been referred to as "the oldest profession." After reading this chapter, can you explain why it might be the oldest form of exploitation or slavery instead of a "profession"?

3. Tiffany is a sad example of how young teens who have been sex trafficked are dying. Look for an organization working to help these young teens and discuss how you might assist them through financial support or by volunteering your time.

4. An outcry from citizens and lawmakers was able to shut down the adult services section of Craigslist. What are some other ways that we as consumers may bring pressure on businesses to help stop sex trafficking?

5. Find a recent news story about someone rescued from sex trafficking and discuss it. What might you do to prevent your own children or others from being trafficked?

7

To the Super Bowl and Beyond

Prostitution is not the oldest business.
Slavery is the oldest business.

—Unknown

As we've seen over and over again, human traffickers value profit over life. It's all about the money. As a result, individuals who are being sex trafficked are not only forced to work the circuit (the city-to-city trek on which pimps move the girls as described in the previous chapter), they're routinely brought into areas hosting big events that cater to a primarily male population. And in that category, one of the most prominent is football's Super Bowl. Super Bowl 2014 was estimated to have brought New York and New Jersey $550 to $600 million in additional revenues for spending in the locale hosting the event.[1] Couple that kind of money with the

147

accompanying party culture, and you have what many traffickers view as an attractive opportunity to market victims.

To usher in Miami's Super Bowl crowd in 2010, a local free publication featured a scantily clad blonde on the front cover with the large caption that read: "Super Blow." Inside was a how-to manual for those rookies looking to buy sex and drugs. The article advertised, "You can have anything you want for the right price. Down here, there's a general understanding that everybody needs something."[2] It went on to say that one could "hire prostitutes of eight races and three sexual orientations, and find a group of people willing to dress up like horses and let you whip them all before dinner." In case the reader was looking for more detailed information, the magazine also offered information on how to determine if your "prostitute" was a cop, decode escort ads, behave in strip clubs, and retrieve the most enjoyment for your money.

Accompanying paid advertisements ensured that Super Bowl tourists would be provided with whatever their hearts desired in other unimaginable ways. If there was ever any question that activities surrounding the Super Bowl are culturally connected with sex trafficking and drugs, this publication erased all doubt.

One of the few positive aspects of such seediness is the opportunity that this yearly convergence of human traffickers presents for law enforcement to rescue victims. That is why in February 2010 I joined a team that began the first anti-trafficking work with the events surrounding the Super Bowl. In partnership with law enforcement and local nonprofits, we organized an outreach to girls being sex trafficked in Miami during the Super Bowl. I have been involved with such efforts for every Super Bowl since.

Armed with missing children flyers, we spent daytime hours canvassing businesses where pimps might bring their girls, including a flea market with a plethora of cheap nail and hair salons, tattoo parlors, lingerie shops, and even booths that would, for the right amount of cash, install a fancy gold tooth. This warehouse in the middle of a shady part of town had everything sex traffickers needed to keep their criminal activities going in style. When I walked into one tattoo booth and set down my clipboard containing missing girls' pictures on the glass case in front of us, the manager's eyes quickly filled with tears and she turned her head. As she composed herself and began looking at the flyers, she recognized several of the missing girls on the posters. We gathered as much detailed information from her as we could and expressed our gratitude. Solid leads like the ones she provided were turned over to the local authorities and became key in recovering many missing and endangered kids that weekend.

During the nights, we walked the streets of South Beach in Miami, which literally crawled with sex-trafficked individuals and their pimps. Our challenge was to find children and teens who were made to dress up and work as sex slaves. These minors being trafficked have been abused, raped, and manipulated into believing that this is all their idea, that this is a choice they are making. And yet our society has labeled them "willing participants in a victimless crime." What a tragedy. Children are being used in the most horrific ways to make money for pimps, whom they often believe are their "boyfriends."

An opportunity for a real conversation with these young victims will likely result in them excitedly declaring their love for the person who is really their trafficker. Considering the brainwashing and sexual and physical abuse these girls have experienced at the hands of their pimps, I sometimes wonder how they have even survived.

The truth is that many have not. According to one study, 65 percent of female sex-trafficking victims reported suffering internal pain, 24 percent experienced head injuries, and 12 percent reported broken bones.[3] And since so many of the missing are never reported, we'll never know just how many lose their lives.

Arizona State University released a study in March of 2014 based on data that was gathered, among other places, in New Jersey and New York during the Super Bowl that took place there in 2014. They found that the Super Bowl or any other large event providing such a concentration of people in an urban area becomes a desirable location for traffickers to bring their victims for commercial sexual exploitation.[4]

Predators versus Potential Victims

On Saturday night before the 2013 Super Bowl in New Orleans, we walked around the party area and watched a woman exit a limousine abruptly. The driver got out and had a conversation with her, trying to talk her into getting back in, but as we were watching from about fifty yards away, we saw her refuse over and over again. As the limo pulled away from the curb, we approached her to see if she needed help. I asked her, "Are you okay?"

"NO!" she replied. "I want to go home!" She was very drunk and didn't want to talk about what had happened, so we didn't pry but began trying to find a ride to get her home safely. In spite of the fact that she had a purse full of cash to pay for a taxi, no taxi driver was willing to take her home, though we tried for about an hour and a half. We enlisted the help of police officers who were working at that corner, and even they couldn't get a taxi to give her a ride.

Finally, as the officers and I discussed the situation, they said that if I was willing to, it might be a good idea for the group I was with to give her a ride home in my rental car. We did just that, and after we delivered her safely to her door, we headed back downtown to party central.

After we dropped her off, our GPS had us drive down a back street that was very seedy. In the darkness, without streetlights, we observed pimps and their victims standing on the sidewalks on either side of the street. With less-than-friendly eyes, they checked us out as we drove by to see if we were a customer cruising down the street for a "date." They gave us a "get outta here" look once they realized we were a carload of obviously sober, middle-aged people observing them with caution.

Just at the end of that street we hit the edge of downtown and ran out of gas. The gas gauge hadn't looked that low, but there was no mistake: the tank was empty. We called AAA and waited for our rescue. While sitting in the car we noticed two very young women at the street corner in front of our car who were trying to hail a cab. They had been partying.

One of them would occasionally walk over to the curb and throw up in the gutter. They were laughing and having a good time, with very little concern about the fact that they couldn't even get a taxi to slow down, much less stop and pick them up. Taxi after taxi passed by as they both raised their arms to hail them.

Then it began. Pimps from a few blocks down had spotted the girls and began to migrate toward them. Like vultures circling their prey, at first they walked by, staring at them lewdly and making rude remarks as they passed. The girls were too drunk to pay much attention to them and continued trying to hail a cab.

At that point the pimps became bolder. They began touching the gals on their upper arms, without pushing them over, just to break the physical barrier of touch. Then they walked around them a couple of times on the sidewalk, and finally one walked straight up to them.

As if out of nowhere, and before the pimp could say much, another young man saw what was happening and walked up and put his arm around one of the girls. As the pimp got close enough to get in the young woman's face, the young man high-fived him and let him know that the girls were with him. The pimp walked off but within five minutes made another attempt. Again the other young man came out of nowhere.

It was about then that AAA arrived with our gas. One of the women in our car got out and told the girls, "Get in the car; we'll give you a ride home."

They quickly scurried into the car, relieved to be with a carload of middle-aged folks who appeared safe. As we drove them to their dorm, the girls told us that they had begun to feel very afraid and didn't know what they were going to do to be safe. There were no police patrolling in that part of town, and the batteries in both of their cell phones were dead.

They confided that they were both nineteen years old and freshmen at Tulane University. As we took them home, they were trembling with fear. With panic in their voices, they said that earlier in the day it had seemed like such a good idea to get fake IDs and party with the Super Bowl crowd.

One admitted, "At first when the pimps started talking to us, it didn't bother me. Then I realized what was happening and I was so scared, and I didn't know what to do."

We began cautioning them (read: "Mom lecturing") as we drove. The magnitude of what they'd narrowly escaped began to soak in.

When we dropped them off at their university dorms, we hugged before they headed inside. I whispered to one of the girls, "Someone was praying for you tonight." She began sobbing, and she uttered through the sobs, "I know who it was . . . it was my grandma." At that, the tears flowed freely—both her tears and mine.

At the 2013 New Orleans Super Bowl, the official numbers that law enforcement released to the press showed there were eighty-five arrests pertaining to human trafficking and five victims of human trafficking officially rescued. Please note, these were arrests and rescues by law enforcement. While our team was connected to law enforcement, we have no claim to these numbers but are honored to have played a small part in working together to stop human trafficking. This number didn't include stories like those young women from Tulane University or others who were not confirmed human trafficking victims. In the end, the numbers aren't important, except that each one represents a precious human being with their own story.

As we drove away from the Tulane campus, I was reminded that the fight we are in to stop human trafficking is real, and that the traffickers are not selective about their victims. Any vulnerable person will do. This game is about traffickers making money.

When I speak with young adults, I caution them that partying may not be safe, even with a friend. It's important to be in a group and to have previously agreed-upon guidelines in order to stay safe.

A Word of Caution

I must give a very loud caution at this point. Going out on the streets at Super Bowl or any other time to locate victims of sex trafficking may seem exciting. I assure you, this type of work is very dangerous and should not be undertaken without prearranged cooperation with specific law enforcement agencies *and* an agreed protocol of how you will cooperate with them. Lone rangers and do-gooders can and should be held responsible by law enforcement if they endanger lives by reckless actions. Such actions can actually cost their own lives as well as the lives of victims and law enforcement officers. Again, never attempt the work I've described above without first having complete cooperation and protocol with local law enforcement.

It's Everywhere

The Super Bowl and other big events are not prerequisites for such human trafficking. In fact, in the years I have been involved in leading anti-trafficking efforts surrounding the Super Bowl, we have seen nationwide awareness rise to an astounding level. This awareness has effected change in that communities are now blanketed with literature and education years before the big event, and law enforcement has effectively stepped up their efforts not just weeks, but months and years leading up to the Super Bowl. The awareness about trafficking surrounding the Super Bowl has caused every state hosting the game for the last several years to strengthen their laws prior to the event, which results in a long-term benefit in the fight against trafficking.

In leading my group's anti-trafficking efforts, I work with state attorneys general, other government officials, law enforcement, and other nonprofits months and even years ahead of time to prepare for our efforts. I often advise them that the best results will be the long-term ones that will change the face of human trafficking in their area.

Regular citizens are much more aware that sex trafficking happens during the Super Bowl than they are that it happens throughout the year in their own communities. Sexual exploitation of human trafficking victims is happening in cities, towns, and rural areas all over this fair country of ours, 365 days a year. America is the richest nation in the world. It stands to reason that traffickers milk the land of plenty where they can reap the biggest profits.

Not all involved in prostitution are being trafficked, but most are doing it against their will,[5] with 89 percent of the prostitutes surveyed in one nine-country study wishing to leave prostitution.[6]

Wanted: Future Sex Slaves

From the malls to Facebook, kids and young women and men are daily targets for human traffickers looking to exploit them sexually. When confronted by these seasoned criminals who excel at molding their message, uninformed targets rarely have a chance. "What you can see, time and time again, is that the predators will adapt their means to whatever the young people are doing— whether it's malls, whether it's ski slopes, whether it's beaches," FBI Deputy Assistant Director Chip Burrus says. "Predators . . . are going to do everything in their power to try to convince young girls and young boys to come with them and enter this particular lifestyle."[7]

The trafficker paints a scenario for the youngsters that minimizes or denies the realities of sex trafficking. He may tell his recruit that others are giving it away for free, or that while everyone gets something for sex—like clothes, dinner, a home—she will get straight cash. (Never mind the fact that *all* of that cash comes back to the trafficker.) He may also play down the fact that she's being sold and will experience the most horrific and torturous life on this planet, telling her instead that having sex for money is just like waiting tables, doing plumbing, or counseling someone. She's not really selling herself, he tells her. She's just providing a service.

Turning Out—Initiation

Every sex-trafficked individual—no matter how young or how old—has a story. Each story is unique, and yet many have tremendous similarities. Each involves a recruitment of sorts, followed by a seasoning and then being turned out. The object of this methodology is to eradicate the victim's identity, deleting any personal self-worth and triggering the abandonment of any sense of entitlement when it comes to dignity, bodily integrity, or choices in life. The seasoning may include exerting control via rapes, beatings, starvation, and taking pornographic photos of the victim that can be used as blackmail, fortifying the pimp's story that this victim has voluntarily chosen to be sexually exploited. Isolation from family and friends makes it easier to control the victim. Then, stripped of any sense of self-esteem, the victim learns obedience to the criminal who has broken her and to anyone he designates as his surrogate.

Dissociation

After being broken in or turned out—and learning her "place" in the process—a trafficked girl or young woman adopts the identity forced upon her and loses any sense of her own humanity and worth. Small wonder. As Vednita Carter and Evelina Giobbe write in the *Hastings Women's Law Journal*, "A girl who enters prostitution at fourteen will have submitted to the sexual demands of four thousand men before she is old enough to drive a car, eight thousand men before she is old enough to vote, and twelve thousand men before she is deemed mature enough to buy a single beer in many states."[8]

It seems that people around the world forced into prostitution share similar coping mechanisms. In her book *Prostitution, Trafficking and Traumatic Stress*, Melissa Farley quotes an Australian victim who says, "When I work my face is expressionless. Of course when I first speak to them, I put on my best pretty-please smile. But in the room I become nothing and nobody. I can only work from below the neck. If I have to think about a service or involve my mind even slightly, I feel dirty. I avoid fantasies. I don't want to participate in their filth."[9]

The message was eerily similar when *Today Show* anchor Meredith Vieira asked Katya,* a survivor of sex trafficking who was trafficked from an Eastern Bloc country to Detroit, what she wanted people to understand about trafficking. "We was really scared.

There was physical abuse on us and they tell us the story about other girls who escape, they bombed their cars, and I was just really scared for my life and my mom's life. . . . I want them to understand, if I have a smile on my face, it doesn't mean I'm here with my own will," she said. "It doesn't mean that I appreciate this job and I want to be here, [but] that it's not for me just easy to leave because I was kept [against my will]."[10]

Reverse Trafficking

Tragically, rescue of trafficking victims in the United States is scant at best, something we will revisit in chapter 8. But for victims of reverse trafficking—a crime trend involving American citizens trafficked to another country—odds of rescue are even slimmer. American girls respond to newspaper classified ads promising modeling, singing, or dancing jobs abroad, only to find out once they arrive in the foreign country that the jobs don't exist. Instead, they're forced into sex trafficking in strip clubs or brothels to repay their debts.

One young dancer from Las Vegas who answered an ad touting a musical in Japan applied and got hired.[11] She would have to leave her three-year-old child behind, but the experience and the money she would be able to bring home would make the two or three months of separation worthwhile.

Instead of the theatrical break she anticipated, however, upon her arrival she was taken to a home where she was beaten and gang-raped for a week and a half. Once her traffickers had broken her will, they put her to work in their brothel. The group that now controlled her said that in order for her to be free, she had to repay all the money they had spent to bring her to Japan. It took her three years to save the required amount. That's when they told her that she had not accounted for the interest and now owed them more.

Luckily, shortly thereafter an open window provided an avenue for escape, and eventually she was able to make her way back to the United States.

Pain, Not Pleasure

Despite the realities, the myth persists that prostitutes, strippers, and porn stars are there because they choose or want to be. Most of the time, this impression of the "wanton woman" is completely false. Usually she has been subjected to someone else's evil and violent deeds and is forced to do what she does.

In truth, even the woman who isn't a victim of human trafficking—at least as I've defined it in this book—but willingly sells her body to strangers doesn't enjoy it. In the overwhelming majority of these instances, the women who "work" in prostitution and pornography do so not because it is some kind of chosen career path but do so simply because they have to eke out a living and don't believe they have alternatives. Many women who have been sex trafficked at a younger age end up "aging out" by their late twenties or early thirties because most sex buyers desire younger victims. If a woman has known no real employment, she may believe prostitution is her only option.

That's just one reason why the arguments to legalize prostitution don't hold up. Legalized prostitution benefits primarily the pimps, brothels, and sex buyers. Amsterdam, a tourist destination in part because of its longtime legal prostitution, has attracted sex traffickers in droves. It might also surprise you to learn that sexual assault becomes more common in areas with a high density of sex businesses.[12] Indeed, Nevada's rate of rape in 2004 was 40.9 per 100,000, higher than the US average (32.2) and significantly higher than many other states.[13]

Finally, Nevada's legalization of prostitution actually encourages sex trafficking instead of eliminating it. In its report of January 2007, the US Department of Justice named Las Vegas one of the seventeen most likely destinations for sex-trafficking victims.[14]

Who's Buying?

Who are the mysterious "buyers of sex"? They are sometimes called "johns," but I prefer not to use that term. Many of us in anti-trafficking work feel that term is too nice of a word and that it doesn't describe what they are. Buyers of sex are those who rent human beings like an object to dehumanize and use them in selfish disrespect, and who more often than not are stimulated by forcing shame, pain, and degradation.[15]

We know from arrest records that they come from every walk of life—doctors, lawyers, cops, teachers, professors, businessmen, politicians, pastors, sports figures, military personnel—and in all shapes and sizes.

Not much press is given to this topic, and in many ways research in this area has just begun. It is impossible to give an exact profile of every sex buyer, but one study found some commonalities. Questionnaires were given to seven hundred men who were arrested while trying to buy street prostitutes in San Francisco, Portland, and Las Vegas to establish whether or not they conceive of sex as a commodity. Some of the commonalities were as follows:

- Median age was 37
- 41 percent were married
- 42 percent had a bachelor's degree
- 35 percent had attended some college
- 81 percent were employed full-time

- 26 percent reported serving in the military
- 64 percent reported purchasing sex at least once in the last twelve months
- Approximately 30 percent watched a pornographic video either a couple of times a month, weekly, or every day[16]

While there is much room for improvement, penalties are being increased for those who are arrested for buying sex, especially if they have purchased a commercial sex act from a minor.

Without this demand for sex as a commodity, there could be no sex trafficking, so toughening up penalties and meting out justice for the demand side of sex trafficking will be key in winning the fight against sex trafficking.

There is a nontraditional deterrent that many cities across the country have adopted to try to prevent sex trafficking and to educate those buying sex. When a first-time offender is arrested for purchasing sex, one option for sentencing may be a diversion program called "john school." The option for the convicted sex buyer to use this program may or may not also include monetary fines and short jail time.

During their school time, which may range from a few hours to multiple Saturdays, they learn about sexually transmitted diseases, the risk of prison time if they get caught again, their role in this vicious and violent crime, where the money they pay for sex really goes, and how sex trafficking destroys the lives of its victims. They hear true stories from law enforcement, prosecutors, and survivors of the torture and degradation of sex trafficking. By the end of the class, the hope is that they will understand that most victims don't want to sell themselves and that as buyers of sex they contribute to the torture, pain, and furtherance of this crime against many who have been forced into prostitution.

Some feel that this form of deterrent is soft on criminals; others feel it is an effective means of reducing demand for victims of sex trafficking. While john schools can be found in many cities of our nation, there are wide ranges of statistics as to how effective they are and the accuracy of their success measurements.

Get Political

In addition to helping the victims we encounter in our everyday lives, we have the opportunity to help keep the multitude of potential and future victims safe. That means lobbying politicians for laws that effectively fight sex trafficking. Many of the laws currently on the books punish the victims—the very people who have been trafficked—instead of the perpetrators who pimp them. Children—that is, those under eighteen years old—are still arrested for being "prostitutes" in many places. Instead of being given services to help them as victims of crime, they are being treated as criminals. When the emphasis is on arresting the victims for selling sex, whether they are children or adults, the incidence of sex trafficking increases.

Compare that to Sweden. In 1999, the country changed its laws to criminalize the purchase of sexual services. Instead of punishing the victims, as we often do in the United States, those who profit from sex trafficking are incarcerated for up to ten years, and those who support it as customers are slapped with fines and/or jail sentences of up to six months. The victims themselves are funneled into social services to get the help they clearly need. By October 2004, five years after the law's enactment, street prostitution had reportedly decreased by at least 30 to 50 percent, and the recruitment of new women for street prostitution had plummeted to almost nothing.[17]

Our legal system has begun to recognize that the majority of prostituted individuals are or have been victims, and that the real criminals are the pimps, along with the mostly male buyers of sex who come from all walks of life, reflect every race, are young and old, rich and poor, married and single.

Sheriff Tom Dart of Cook County, Illinois, has directed his department to model their approach similarly to Sweden's system. Accordingly, resources previously directed at the endless cycle of arresting, releasing, and rearresting those practicing prostitution have been shifted to target the crime's perpetrators instead. Local law enforcement now arrests pimps and sex buyers and impounds their cars.

Additionally, he founded the "National Day of Johns Arrests." It actually is a series of days on which various law enforcement agencies from around the country focus their efforts on arresting sex buyers and traffickers. "Sex trafficking continues to destroy countless lives, and deterring demand for paid sex is the most effective way to eradicate this reprehensible underground trade," said Sheriff Dart. "I'm proud of the fantastic results among this growing national coalition as we forcefully deliver the message that prostitution is not a victimless crime."[18]

Prostituted individuals, instead of being incarcerated, are referred to social services for support and assistance so they can recover physically, emotionally, and financially from the traumatic and inhumane experiences they have suffered. They need the support. We don't assume anyone wants to be beaten or sexually abused. Why has our society insisted on the "right" of an individual to be prostituted or sex trafficked?

A study by the Chicago Coalition for the Homeless revealed that of 235 women in Cook County Jail on October 31, 2001, "82 percent of the women had been physically assaulted; 83 percent had been threatened with a weapon, [and] 68 percent had been raped while working as a prostitute."[19] The 2005 Trafficking in Persons Report stated that 70 to 95 percent of women in prostitution were physically assaulted.[20] While no system is perfect, I believe that actions such as Sheriff Dart's will be key in the efforts to stop the sale of humans in the United States.

Words of Respect

As you have read this book so far, you may have noticed the words I use to describe different aspects of sex trafficking are different from some you have previously heard. In my work, I have seen the pain that commonly used words in our society have caused victims and survivors as well as those of us engaged in the fight against trafficking. The way we describe people, places, or things shapes how we feel and how we act toward them. As one training resource put it, "Words are powerful. They define the limits or boundaries around ideas, beliefs, and interactions. The way you talk about something becomes the way you think about it, just as the way you identify someone becomes the way you think about that person."[21]

I would like to summarize the concepts found in an excellent resource called the chart of "Preferred Terminology for Sex Trafficking and Prostitution" and its preface by Lisa L. Thompson.[22]

When referring to sex trafficking, I call it what it is: *sex trafficking*. It is not a legal industry, so I don't use words like *sex industry* or *sex work*. It is a criminal enterprise built on shattering lives in the most horrific ways for monetary gain. The only time I use the words "legal sex industry" are when referring to a business for which one can go to the county or state licensing bureau and obtain a legal permit to do business, such as strip clubs, lingerie shops, and sex shops. However, as I have noted earlier, the activities occurring in these businesses do not always reflect the work that they were licensed to do in that business.

Most of us have experienced name-calling in our lifetime. No one wants to be labeled by derogatory terms or called names that are pejorative. Respect for victims and survivors requires that while properly conveying the activity that is occurring to them, we communicate that it is an experience inflicted on an individual, not a state of being.

Certainly those who have been victimized by sex trafficking deserve our effort to respect them with our words. Therefore, when I refer to someone who is being sex trafficked, I refer to them as a sex-trafficked woman, man, child, or individual. Words that should not be used are *prostitute*, *ho*, or any other words that are degrading or that signify that the activities they are engaged in are simply a reflection of their personal choices.

If they are still being sex trafficked, I refer to them as a victim of sex trafficking, but if they are out of the life, even for a moment, I refer to them as a survivor.

As I recently worked with law enforcement in helping a survivor who was rescued from sex trafficking in a sting operation, I was trying to encourage her with that line of thinking. The young woman hung her head in shame and told me, "I can't believe what I have become. I never intended to be a prostitute." I gently said to her, "You are not a prostitute. Do not ever let anyone call you a prostitute. You have been sex trafficked, and you didn't deserve what happened to you. You are a strong survivor and a precious and valuable child of God."

As I said that, she sat up a little in her chair, and her countenance changed from shame to wanting to believe she was valuable and didn't deserve what happened to her. It is a long and very difficult road of recovery for survivors, and I admire the tremendous courage it takes each precious and valuable person to begin and continue on that road.

Common words for those who purchase commercial sex are *john*, *trick*, *date*, *client*, *customer*, or *hobbyist*. In my mind those words communicate respect for the criminal activity of someone who is breaking the law by paying money to rent and abuse another human being. Words I use are *sex buyer*, *prostitutor*, *purchaser of commercial sex*, *perpetrator*, or *criminal*.

For sex traffickers, I try to avoid the use of the word *pimp* unless I have previously explained the disgusting role of what our society calls a pimp. I use words such as *perpetrator*, *trafficker*, *captor*, and *criminal*. These words accurately describe the role of those involved in sexual exploitation of others.

A part of healing the pain, degradation, and hurt imparted by sex trafficking is all of us learning to use words that communicate truth in a manner that accurately describes the activity while respecting individuals who have been trafficked and accurately naming that activity as a crime.

This work is a delicate balance of pressing forward to get the job done while respecting the journey and boundaries of all those we encounter along the way.

For Discussion

1. What is it about the celebrations around the Super Bowl and other large events that attract sex traffickers to bring victims to be sold there?

2. What is reverse trafficking? How do those traffickers generally recruit American citizens, and how might that be prevented?

3. Who are the buyers of commercial sex? What do you think might help reduce the demand for commercial sex?

4. Contact a local legislator to find out what your state's laws are surrounding human trafficking. How might those laws be improved in your area?

5. Find a recent news story about someone rescued from sex trafficking and discuss it. How did the media use or not use appropriate language around the case? What wording might you have changed to show respect for victims/survivors and expose the crime or criminals involved?

8

Why Victims Stay

If I could have convinced more slaves that they were slaves,
I could have freed thousands more.

—Harriet Tubman

August 23, 1973, began like any other day for Kristin Enmark, a
petite twenty-three-year-old woman with sassy short brown hair
from Stockholm, Sweden.[1] She had already plunged into her work
as a bank stenographer, a job she generally liked, when she heard
a commotion out in the lobby area. She looked up to see a man
with an afro wig and sunglasses pull out a machine gun, which he
fired in the air. She and the forty other terrified bank employees
and customers ducked for cover or ran out of the building.

"The party has only started," the man shouted in English.[2]

Police were called and responded quickly. As they walked into
the bank, the gunman, Jan Erik Olsson, shot and injured one of

the two policemen. He ordered the other officer to sit in a chair and "sing something." The officer managed to croak out a few bars of "Lonesome Cowboy."[3]

Olsson, who had intended to rob the bank, took hostage four bank employees—three women (Kristin, Birgitta Lundblad, and Elisabeth Oldgren) and one man (Sven Safstrom). He ordered a male bookkeeper to tie their hands behind their backs. He made several demands of police, including that they bring a friend of his, Clark Olofsson, from prison where he was serving a sentence for another crime.[4]

Kristin would later learn that in addition to the machine gun, Olsson had brought reserve ammunition, plastic explosives (which he had expertise in using), blasting caps, a knife, and a radio. He meant business. Even though he had botched the bank robbery, he remained determined to make something out of what was left.[5]

Over the next days, Kristin and the other hostages would come to know Olsson and Olofsson not only as strangers who held the key to their life and death, but as the men who controlled everything about their lives, including where and what they ate, where and how much they slept, where and when they went to the bathroom, and how safe they felt.

Curiously, in short order this also gave the gunmen control over their hostages' emotions. In a matter of hours, Kristin and the others had so bonded to the gunmen that they believed the two men were actually protecting them from law enforcement, which they now viewed as a threat. Further, the hostages had become protective of the gunmen, whom they viewed as saviors rather than captors. The phenomenon would become known as "Stockholm syndrome."[6]

For five days, as the hostages were trapped in the bank vault with their captors, they had explosives strapped to them, witnessed the robbers shoot two more officers who were trying to rescue them by drilling a hole in the top of the bank vault, and had their lives threatened daily.[7] Yet by the second day of captivity, when Olsson gave a commissioner permission to come in and check on the welfare of the hostages, the hostages showed hostility toward the commissioner. He said that none of the hostages had any requests for him and he could detect no imploring looks. There seemed to be a cordial disposition between the hostages and their captors; Olofsson even stood with his arm around Kristin and Elisabeth's shoulders in seeming camaraderie. To Kristin, who practically curled up her lip at the commissioner, the disdain she felt toward him made perfect sense. His presence jeopardized the safety she felt with Olsson and Olofsson.

Officials had agreed to almost all of Olsson's requests, including bulletproof jackets, food, money, two pistols, and a fast getaway car. The only nonnegotiable item was that the captors not be allowed to take the hostages with them when they left, even though all four had petitioned to leave with their captors.[8]

Later that day, Kristin had the opportunity to call Prime Minister Olof Palme. Although she didn't know him personally, they spoke for forty-two minutes. She felt that if she could convince him that they were really safe here with Olsson, the officials would let them all leave together.

"I am really disappointed," she told the prime minister. "I think you are sitting there playing checkers with our lives. I fully trust Clark [Olofsson] and the robber [Olsson]. I am not desperate. They haven't done a thing to us. On the contrary, they have been very nice. But you know, Olof, what I'm scared of is that the police will attack and cause us to die."[9]

"The police will not harm you," the prime minister replied. "Can you believe that?"

"You must forgive me, but in this situation I don't believe it."

"I think that's terribly unfair. Here are a great many policemen risking their lives, who have not moved aggressively in all this time. The purpose, of course, is to protect you."

"Of course they can't attack us . . . [Olsson] is sitting here and he's protecting us from the police."

The phone call ended with Kristin sarcastically telling Prime Minister Palme, "Thanks for the help!"[10]

Kristin and the other hostages were fully convinced by the second day that their safety was dependent on the robbers, not the police.

The third day, after negotiations to have the police send in food and other supplies had fallen through, Olsson wrote the following note: "The girls have begun to believe that police intend to sacrifice them and are only looking for an excuse to justify the massacre later on. The girls believe that the police will make sure it was we who started it and that the police simply defended themselves, so that they can afterward regret that everyone was killed."[11]

Later, when the ordeal was over, another hostage, Birgitta Lundblad, was asked if the note was accurate. She indicated it was. "We were facing two threats, and one was all we could possibly handle. About the robber's threat we could do nothing—he was armed and we were with him. But we weren't with the police. We imagined we could protect ourselves against them. To imagine that, of course, meant believing in Jan [Olsson]."[12]

Kristin and Olofsson formed a special bond. One night she awoke from a nightmare screaming, "Don't! Don't!" Olofsson immediately rushed to her side, consoling her until she was herself again. She told police after the rescue that she and Olofsson held hands. "Perhaps it sounds a little like a cliché, but Clark [Olofsson] gave me tenderness. . . . It made me feel enormously secure. It was what I needed."[13]

Even at the end of the ordeal, after five days in the vault, Kristin tried to defend her captors as they were to exit. Police had sprayed tear gas in the vault, causing choking and vomiting inside.

"We give up. Let us out!" Olsson hollered.[14]

"Hostages first," the police replied.

Kristin refused. "No, Jan [Olsson] and Clark [Olofsson] go first. You'll gun them down if we [leave first]," she yelled.[15]

As the vault door was opened, the hostages and their captors said their good-byes. The women kissed their captors, and the male hostage shook their hands. Then all six came out of the vault, perpetrators first.

The hostages were to be taken to a medical center to be evaluated. Kristin, however, was so worried about the men who had taken her hostage that she refused to lie on her stretcher. As she craned her neck to see them and spotted Olofsson being interrogated by police, she called out, "Clark, I'll see you again!"[16] And she did. Although Olofsson had to go back to prison to serve the rest of his term, which amounted to almost six years, Kristin and her family would become longtime friends with him and his family.

After their rescue, the hostages reiterated their claims that during the ordeal they were more frightened of the police than of the men who had taken them hostage. They had clearly identified with their captors and created an alternate reality for themselves.

In the days and months following the rescue, all of the hostages remained loyal to the perpetrators. One hostage even accused the psychiatrists of trying to brainwash them to turn against their captors.[17] When the hostages were finally willing to testify against their captors a full six months after the holdup, Olsson was sentenced to ten years as the instigator of the ordeal.

Bonding with the Perpetrator

The Stockholm syndrome[18]—this identification of victims with their abusers—has been linked to many famous kidnapping and hostage cases in the United States, including Patty Hearst, Elizabeth Smart, Shawn Hornbeck, and Jaycee Dugard. After Dugard's rescue in August 2009, kidnapping survivor Shawn Hornbeck was asked why he thought she had never escaped. "You're brainwashed," he said. "It's as simple as that. I know people use that term a lot, but that's what happens to you. It's like you are on autopilot, only someone else is controlling all the switches. They control every little, minute detail in your life. Everything."[19] Attachment between hostage and captor is the rule rather than the exception. The goal of the perpetrator is to instill in the victim not just fear of death but gratitude for being allowed to live.

Others who may experience Stockholm syndrome include cult members, concentration camp prisoners, prisoners of war, abused children, incest victims, victims of battering or psychological abuse, and those in intimidating or controlling relationships. Readers who have experienced domestic violence may understand the feelings of Stockholm syndrome all too well, since power and control are the hallmarks of abusive relationships.

The human mind and heart are complex. But for the purposes of this book, this story helps us witness the phenomenon of four victims held in a bank vault by robbers whom they had never previously met. In a matter of hours, the victims felt safer and more protected with their captors than with the police. Possibly this story can also help us understand why human trafficking victims, some who have been groomed by their captors for months or years, can remain loyal to—and return to—those captors, even when that seemingly makes no sense to an outsider.

The same dynamic that made the hostages in that Stockholm bank feel more trust and loyalty toward the robbers holding them captive than they did toward the police keeps victims from escaping traffickers who have enslaved them. Stockholm syndrome may finally have been identified in 1973, but its effects are nothing new.

Harriet Tubman, that courageous and saintly woman who believed that, like Moses, she had to lead her people to freedom, once said, "If I could have convinced more slaves that they were slaves, I could have freed thousands more."[20]

I would say the same holds true today. I know many survivors of sex trafficking who have experienced torturous abuse from their pimps, yet they remain convinced, even years after they escape the life, that their involvement in prostitution was their own idea, until they finally sort through the emotions and facts. Trauma bonds are a powerful shackle.

How does this kind of brainwashing occur? It usually starts with abuse, a common occurrence in every type of human trafficking case. Captors and/or abusers make a practice of controlling their victims through fear and intimidation, usually starting with verbal abuse. When a girl is soliciting sex buyers on the track (streets where soliciting is commonly done) and she hasn't picked up a customer in a little while, her pimp will frequently drive up and have her get in the car. "Get out there and make me some money," he screams at her. (That's the censored version.) Then he may tell her that she's worthless and call her names that would not be appropriate to print here. He may threaten her with a beating or other physical abuse.

The threats are all too real. The violence, which impacts 86 percent of US women and girls sold into prostitution, according to one survey,[21] varies from slaps and punches to more overt physical force and even horrific torture. This physical abuse has a psychological component as well. It encourages victims to cooperate, since they seek to avoid being punished for infractions like bringing home less money than their quota.

It's also not uncommon for perpetrators to punish one victim in front of another to reinforce the fear that they are capable of inflicting severe injury or even death. This extreme physical abuse usually occurs when a victim attempts to resist the captors' control.

By making an example of the rebel, even to the point of killing her, they can cement the others' cooperation, which ultimately will enhance the traffickers' profits despite the loss of an income-generating body.[22]

Beating a slave's friend or co-slave instead of the person who supposedly committed the misdeed is another powerful tool when it comes to controlling victims. Threatening a woman's family can be even more effective. Young girls who are sex trafficked are commonly told by their pimp that he will go get a cherished little sister, cousin, or some other young and innocent girl she knows and loves, and force her into prostitution if she doesn't do what he wants. Threats of harm might also be made against the victims' parents, friends, or children. The Las Vegas dancer trafficked to Japan, whose story I shared in chapter 7, was successfully kept in check for years by regular reminders from her traffickers that they knew where her daughter lived and would have people "take care of her family" if she didn't obey them. To keep her family safe, she did what she was told to do. She knew all too well that her registration form contained all the information they would need to execute their threats.

Getting a girl hooked on drugs, a common tactic in sex trafficking, is another way that traffickers gain cooperation and loyalty from their victims. As mentioned in chapter 1, in our small town there are credible reports of young homeless girls waking up in the middle of the night with needles in their arms. A short time later they disappear from the homeless camp. Rumor has it that they are now with traffickers, who control them completely simply by giving or withholding drugs. Once victims become addicts, they will do anything to get the drugs they crave. As an added incentive, traffickers then hold out a carrot: the more money a victim brings in, the better drugs she or he will be given.

As we saw with Kristin in the Stockholm bank, eventually the lack of control over one's own life creates a strange bonding—and

174

even a sense of safety—with one's captor. That explains why traffickers such as pimps can actually control their victims by threatening to leave them. In addition, captors go to great lengths to convince their victims that no one would want to help them even if they asked. Victims are told that police will not believe them, that the police are corrupt, that the trafficker has links to the police, or that the victim is at a legal disadvantage in some way and will be arrested. Eventually, victims come to fear police involvement just as Kristin did and to see their captor as the person who is protecting them from law enforcement or from others who might have been able to assist in their escape. Indeed, in an effort to survive, that's how twisted the mind can become.

It is particularly easy for traffickers to convince people who are not US citizens that they'll be deported if they try to escape their captivity. For many victims, deportation and the shame of returning to their homeland in this manner cause them to believe that staying under the existing slavery is a better option. Others simply fear an outside world and legal system about which they know nothing.

Captors of both foreign-born nationals and US citizens feed this fear and rehearse a script, instructing their victims what to say in case the law does catch up with them. These traffickers know the questions the police will likely ask, and victims are trained to answer in such a way that the perpetrator is not implicated. This scripting, as it's called, is enforced by the other means of control discussed in this chapter, including threats to the victims and their loved ones.

Why Victims Don't Run

There are a host of other reasons—most of which are also symptoms of Stockholm syndrome—that explain why human trafficking victims may not try to escape even when the door is unlocked and the coast is clear:

- Victims are hypervigilant with respect to a captor's needs or beliefs, and they identify with the captor's perspective on the world. They experience intense gratefulness for small kindnesses (such as the captor/abuser not administering a beating when expected) because the captor/abuser holds the power of life and death over them. This triggers a sense of dependence and helplessness.

- Most human trafficking victims don't have friends or family nearby. This holds just as true for victims of forced labor as it does for sex-trafficked victims. As we saw in the last chapter, pimps often keep the girls on what is called the circuit, moving them from place to place every few days or weeks. This may be within a city or from city to city. Either way, the motivation is to keep them from setting up alliances with other girls or with customers who could facilitate escape. It also helps keep the victims disoriented. Prostituted individuals commonly ask "Where am I?" once they've escaped or been rescued. Not knowing what city, state, or even what country they are in adds to the difficulty of leaving.

- One of the telltale signs of human trafficking is that the trafficker often has possession of the victim's identification, driver's license, social security card, passport, etc. In the Las Vegas dancer's case, the woman who met her at the airport said that Japan was experiencing a lot of trouble with identity theft and advised that the dancer hand over all her documents—including her passport and visa—for safekeeping. Stripping away these tangible forms of identification makes it that much more difficult for victims to leave or to seek assistance.

- Dishonesty feeds on honest people who feel they owe their captor something. People who are in debt bondage—whether picking tomatoes or being sexually trafficked—often feel that they can't leave because of their debt to the very person who's stealing their soul. Since the victim has most often been duped into becoming involved with the trafficker—to say nothing of the fact that the financial charges incurred have been exaggerated—that sense of moral obligation is as misguided as it is immobilizing.

- Even if a victim wants to leave and has the opportunity to escape, the fear of reprisal against their loved ones—or themselves if they are ever found by their captor—may convince them to stay. Victims may know from experience with the captor/abuser that they will be found. And they may believe that if they are found, the consequences would be worse for them than if they had never left. Ultimately, the fear of what could happen if they leave can become much greater than the fear of what has happened or is happening to them in captivity. The irony here is that even knowing all of the above, victims may still find a way to deny their captor's true nature in order to shield themselves from their reality.

- Language barriers, cultural differences, and a basic lack of understanding about victims' rights and available services will keep many human trafficking victims from even thinking about trying to flee.

- In addition, most human trafficking victims suffer from post-traumatic stress disorder (PTSD). According to the American Psychiatric Association, the condition may occur when a person has experienced extreme traumatic stressors involving "direct personal experience of an event that involves actual or threatened death or serious injury, or other threat to one's physical integrity; or witnessing an event that involves death, injury, or a threat to the physical integrity of another person; or learning about unexpected or violent death, serious harm, or threat of death or injury experienced by a family member or other close associate." The symptoms of PTSD can include flashbacks—mentally reliving the horrors they experienced during their life of captivity—as well as the avoidance of stimuli associated with the trauma. Victims of PTSD can also experience difficulty falling or staying asleep, anger, and hypervigilance. By definition, the symptoms of PTSD can last for years, and they can cause serious problems in social, occupational, or other important areas of everyday life (for example, problems at work and in personal relationships).[23]

Shaking the Syndrome

Fortunately, some human trafficking victims do manage to shake the Stockholm syndrome and break the chains of human trafficking. Kendall Simmons was a strong student from a good home, whose parents cared about her in all the right ways.[24] But that's not always enough to immunize a young person against the persuasions of the wrong boy. So when Kendall's boyfriend of three months, Darren "DJ" Evans, was kicked out of his mother's home, she moved out of her parents' home and into DJ's car to live with him.

Within days, he entreated her to sell her body. "Baby, we need money," he told her. "Please, baby, do it for me."[25]

She believed she was in love with DJ, so she did what he asked and started walking the strip, turning up to twenty-five tricks a day. She was just sixteen.

Things soon went from bad to worse when DJ began beating her. Each day she headed off to high school wearing sunglasses to hide a black eye or trying to walk without the limp that a beating had induced. As soon as classes were out, she hit the streets to earn money that she was required to bring back to DJ.

Kendall knew that DJ was an alcoholic. She knew he was abusive and controlling. Yet she believed she was in love with him and that he would eventually change his behavior. She believed they would live happily ever after. It took a year for her to decide that she had had enough and that she was ready to go back to her loving family. "I always had a family that I could run back to," she told a reporter. "But I'm rare. I know there's a lot of girls out there that don't have families like mine."[26]

The day after Kendall told DJ she was leaving him for good and actually moved out, he called her at her parents' home and begged to come see her. She agreed. She wanted to show him and herself that she was strong now. The decision nearly cost Kendall her life.

DJ strangled and kicked her, tortured and humiliated her, including requiring her to bark like a dog in order to get a glass of water. Fortunately, she was able to call 911 before he broke her cell phone in half. When the police came, the strangulation marks on her neck were all the evidence they needed to arrest DJ, who subsequently pled guilty to second-degree assault and promoting prostitution. Prostitution? At sixteen, Kendall was not a prostitute but a victim of human trafficking. DJ was sentenced to eight years in prison.

Kendall proved to be a courageous and determined survivor. With the support of her family, she graduated with her high school class and went on to community college in a nearby town. She's majoring in criminal justice and hopes to one day join law enforcement as a detective or an investigator.[27]

Healing after Victimization

As Kendall's and other survivors' families know, rescue is the beginning, not the end of the healing for the victim. There are often lasting mental and physical health issues in addition to the emotional challenges.

Because of the extent of terror and abuse trafficking victims have experienced, there is much work to be done before they can reenter normal life. This is especially true of sex-trafficking victims whose self-image has been systematically stripped away. Victims have usually been ostracized from their friends and family by their perpetrators and/or as a survival mechanism. Likewise, it is hard for victims to return to normal life because they feel everyone knows what happened to them and are embarrassed and afraid of being exposed.

In addition, victims will often take on their abuser's perspective during captivity as part of the bonding with captors mentioned earlier in this chapter. So in addition to not wanting to leave their traffickers, after a period of time victims may come to share their captors' belief systems. These new beliefs can differ drastically from their previous convictions and may include believing that their parents, family, and friends never really loved them like their captor/abuser does or that they cannot survive without their captor/abuser. Victims have been known to threaten their family and friends with restraining orders if they continue to "interfere" or try to help them escape their situation.

Trapped in the Life

Having been stripped of their self-image to the point of adopting an alien set of values, and fearing rejection for what they believe they have now become, some victims of sex trafficking who are rescued won't break free from that kind of life. Since most lack education and job skills, a percentage will inevitably return to the "work" they now believe is their only option instead of remaining in safety.

Breaking free from sex trafficking can be especially difficult for juveniles, virtually all of whom are pimp controlled. Built of desperation and fear, the bonds they form with their pimps can be seemingly impossible to break. This can be particularly true for the young girl who believes she's in love with the very man who is pimping her out. "The problem is that there is no methadone for a bad relationship," says Rachel Lloyd, who was sexually exploited as a child and who is now the director of Girls Educational and Mentoring Services (GEMS), a program in New York that helps girls escape and stay away from the lives they've led.[28] That helps explain why some girls continue "working" for pimps even after the pimps are incarcerated.

Giving Help and Shelter

Despite the fact that only the most effective treatment will help the estimated 100,000 child victims of sex trafficking[29] reclaim their lives, there are way too few residential treatment centers in the United States for sex-trafficked children.

Consider the horrific physical, emotional, and even spiritual damage that can occur to a child who has been subject to crimes like rapes, beatings, brainwashing, and torture for any period of time. Then one day they are rescued, maybe even against their will. They can't be sent back to go to school with the friends they knew before they were subjected to "the life." They need specialized, caring treatment from those who understand this trauma. The challenge is, there are not enough resources available.

While social service organizations seem to be developing a better understanding of the specific needs of teens rescued from sex trafficking, putting a victim in a traditional foster home hasn't been the best solution. Children and teens subjected to commercial sexual exploitation have been conditioned by their pimps to escape from a foster home as soon as they get a chance. That can happen as quickly as entering the front door and walking through the kitchen and out the back door. These youngsters need special services tailored to address the specific abuses and brainwashing they have experienced while being sex trafficked.

As of the time I am writing this book, I know of multiple shelters in the works that plan to tackle these specific needs. I earnestly pray many more shelters will soon be available and that they can be generous with the services and unconditional love that will be imperative when it comes to giving these precious young beings the new start they deserve. These victims and survivors are our kids, and they deserve a helping hand so they can live their lives to the fullest.

Don't Let Them Get Away with This

Human trafficking and slavery thrive in ignorance, silence, and secrecy. But ordinary people like you and me can protest and in a united voice say, "No more!" We owe it to the victims as well as to ourselves not to turn away but to speak out instead.

Jacobo Timmerman, who was a political prisoner during the Holocaust, says, "The Holocaust will be understood not so much for the number of victims as for the magnitude of silence. And what obsesses me the most is the repetition of silence."[30] We all have the opportunity to speak up and not let silence happen during this modern-day atrocity.

Since I became aware of the injustices, the horrors, and the atrocities human traffickers and slave masters commit every day, I've joined countless others who can't keep quiet. And while I don't spend my every waking moment talking to people about human trafficking, I regularly look for opportunities to open people's eyes and help them to understand that these things are happening every day and everywhere—sometimes right under our own noses. I invite you to join the movement and do the same.

Speak up about modern slavery to people you know—your friends, your family members, the leaders in your communities or church, or anyone who is willing to listen.

January 11 is National Human Trafficking Awareness Day. A multitude of events held across the nation on or around that day are designed to raise awareness about human trafficking. Looking for an event to attend, support, or even to volunteer at could be a way for you to engage with others in the fight against human trafficking.

Additionally, once a year, faith-based organizations dedicate a Sunday and a weekend of prayer to anti–human trafficking efforts. These events communicate a message: *I will not tolerate any child of God in my neighborhood, in my backyard, or in my sphere of influence to be trafficked, to be sold, or to be used.* If you are part of a faith-based group, ask them to join the movement to stop slavery in our nation as part of these events and others.

Speak to your local law enforcement and social service agencies, to state and federal agencies, and to state and national leaders, including your own state and federal legislators and others who can make a big difference.

And when you see ads in publications that tolerate things that undergird human trafficking, make your voice heard and protest vigorously. At the Super Bowl, many people sent letters and emails of complaint not only to the magazine mentioned in chapter 7 that ran exploitative sex ads but also to many mainstream corporations that advertised in the magazine. Mainstream companies do not like that kind of spotlight and will usually pressure the publication in question to change its policies.

All a perpetrator asks is that we remain silent. I have vowed to raise my voice about modern slavery as long as I have breath. Take a pledge to break that silence and make as much noise about the atrocity of human trafficking as you can. Because as long as one of us is enslaved, none of us is truly free.

For Discussion

1. What does Stockholm syndrome have to do with modern slavery?

2. Discuss a news story where the victim seems to have bonded with his or her captor. Why do you think the victim may not have escaped when it seemed he or she had opportunities?

3. Families and friends of Stockholm syndrome victims can help by being available to the victim without bad-mouthing the perpetrator to them. How might one support a loved one who is trapped in human trafficking, domestic violence, or other such situations, while still respecting his or her boundaries and without endangering him or her?

4. Harriet Tubman said she could have rescued many more slaves if she could have convinced them they were slaves. If she had that dilemma when slavery was named as such, discuss the difficulty a victim experiences today in escaping modern slavery.

5. How might you help your church or faith-based group promote awareness about human trafficking? How might you personally promote awareness?

9

Wolves in Sheep's Clothing

Sadly, our pop culture—which is exported around the world—glamorizes the role of the pimp, which promotes sex trafficking.

—Mark Lagon

It's an extreme uphill battle for trafficking survivors of any age to move past the horrors of captivity—the months or years of terror, abuse, neglect, pain, subjugation, torture, and humiliation—and live normal, healthy, productive lives. The resulting deep, lasting scars might seem beyond healing, but there are numerous stories of miraculous recoveries. While both victims and traffickers are human beings with value, we must never lose sight of who is the criminal and who is the victim, nor of the need for vigorous prosecution of crimes committed as well as services for survivors. However, to add to the complexity of this crime, all too often perpetrators were once victims. Hurting people hurt people. Until we can compassionately and wisely bring healing to a world of hurting, this crime and others will reproduce.[1]

Hurting People Hurt People

By the time Jason Foster[*2] was in his midtwenties, his father, although it brought him enormous pain, prayed agonizingly for Jason to be removed from this earth because he was hurting so many people with his life choices. The prayers hadn't started out that way. Neither had Jason.

Jason grew up in one of the nicer neighborhoods in Salem, Oregon. His dad, a doctor, and his mom, a stay-at-home mother, were loving parents who strove to provide their two sons with everything they needed to succeed. They also tried to be good neighbors and were active in the community. The couple went to church every Sunday and lived what they believed in their family and community. In short, they had a good reputation and it was well earned.

Jason was a sweet young boy who got along well with others. In addition, he was smart, strong, athletically gifted, and a natural leader. He had it all going for him. There was no reason to question the bright future this young man would have, unless one knew that as a preschooler he had fallen victim to sexual abuse that would change the course of his life.

Jason and his friend Debbie* regularly played out in the forest behind his house, enjoying the simple pleasures of childhood. Childhood dreams that live in a child's mind can transform a simple tree fort into a spaceship. The bicycle without training wheels becomes a race car. And the baseball hit over the backyard fence becomes the grand slam that wins the World Series.

In Debbie's world, however, life wasn't so simple or so pure. Her parents not only had become involved in pornography, they had involved their little girl. Out of her hurt came Jason's. In the midst of their play, she would insist that Jason go with her to the bathroom to perform the sexual acts that her parents had introduced to her.

Jason never felt comfortable with what happened in that bathroom. "Can't we just hug?" he protested. That is how he had been taught to show affection. Instead of agreeing, Debbie threatened to tell Jason's parents about what they'd been doing if he refused to participate in their sexual game.

Years later, Jason still doesn't know why he didn't just call the girl's bluff. In hindsight, she certainly had more to lose than he did. But he was ashamed and he was scared. So he continued to comply with the abuse, which in his words would become "a cornerstone of the person that I [became]."

By puberty, feelings of guilt about the abuse turned to anger. He thought he could handle his feelings, but they were handling him. "I hadn't told anybody," he says. "I had no intention of ever telling anybody that type of a thing, especially being a boy." When the anger boiled over, he turned violent, hurting himself and others without a second thought.

At age fourteen, Jason began experimenting with drugs and alcohol. He found that alcohol made him "comfortably numb." Since he still hadn't told his parents about what had happened—let alone asked anyone for help—the attempts to self-medicate helped him get through the day.

When his parents realized that Jason was experiencing more than just normal teenage rebellion, they did everything they could to help him regain control of his behaviors. They talked with him and grounded him and took away privileges, trying to provide an even balance of love and discipline with boundaries, but nothing seemed to work. Finally, they sent him to a boarding school where he nearly died of an overdose. The boarding school expelled him and sent him home.

His parents refused to give up on their son. Recognizing that he had a substance abuse problem, they admitted him to the best adolescent recovery program they could find. At sixteen, when most kids were trying to be on their best behavior so their parents would let them get their driver's license, Jason was in his first lockup. He felt hurt, betrayed, and even angrier than before.

Rehab did not bring Jason around. Instead, in an attempt to regain the power that had been stripped from him as a child, he careened from doing dangerous drugs to engaging in dangerous activities. He quickly graduated from buying drugs to robbing drug dealers of the product they were illegally selling to others. "What could they do?" he reasoned. "Call the cops on me?" Knowing that he had hurt someone else—in essence sharing the misery—helped ease the pain he carried inside. If he was going to feel such hurt all the time, then others should as well.

Ultimately, however, what he really sought was a sense of control. He would find that control at age fifteen, not through healthy avenues but through a pimp who had chosen to hang out at Jason's school. The pimp was recruiting new girls for his "stable," a term used in trafficking circles for the group of victims a pimp is selling.

Parents sending their upper-middle-class kids to what was at that time the newest and arguably the nicest high school in Salem never dreamed their children could potentially meet a pimp on the premises who would change their lives. But no one seemed to question the presence of this older guy draped in gold jewelry who regularly drove a different, expensive car.

The other kids at school steered clear of Devin,* the pimp. Not Jason. Like a bee to honey, he went straight up to Devin. Before long, the two had become friends. Jason's charisma and charm soon won him favor with the other pimps with whom Devin hung out, and Jason was embraced and accepted into the pimp family. Their lifestyle fascinated him as much as the control they exerted over the girls intrigued and appealed to him. Before long, he didn't just want to witness their way of life, he wanted to share it. Finally, being the one in power could help him forget about what had happened during his childhood.

The pimp family schooled Jason in their ways, and soon he turned out his first girl, Claire,* the girl he had been dating. He had painted her a picture of the life they would share together, telling her that if she really cared about him, she would do this for him. Eventually she agreed, without even asking how the money would be split. That was fine with Jason. He had no intention of sharing with Claire a dime of the money she earned.

Just as he had planned, Jason began to drop off Claire on "dates" and then pocketed the money she brought back. She would be the first of scores of girls who sold their bodies and lined his pockets with 100 percent of their earnings.

Over the years that followed, Jason's life plummeted into deeper destruction. In addition to becoming a full-fledged pimp, he committed crimes involving drugs, weapons, and stolen property. It was all part of "the game," as pimping is known, that Jason had chosen as a lifestyle.

For the next fourteen years, in between prison stints, Jason pimped girls on the streets, in car lots, and in some of the most famous brothels in Nevada. He lived life as fast and as fearlessly as he could, becoming a renowned rap artist in the process. But even after many years, he still hadn't found that "high" that he was seeking. No matter what he did—pimping girls, enjoying their earnings, rapping and cutting albums, becoming known in the underworld as the notorious young white guy who had excelled in pimping and rapping—he felt increasingly empty and unhappy.

He was leading a life of desperation, and he knew it. On two separate occasions when he felt he had hit bottom, Jason called his parents in tears. Each of those points of despair brought him a little closer to getting out of the low life to which he had sunk. He knew what he needed to do, starting with getting away from the booze he knew was killing him. He just couldn't do it alone.

At last, Jason says, he prayed. He was powerless to quit drinking, he admitted as he prayed, and needed help. The next day, despite having consumed copious amounts of alcohol, he awoke feeling fresher than he had in years. He took it as a sign that God was with him. In that instant, he gave up alcohol. He has remained alcohol-free to this day, which amounts to over a decade.

But not using alcohol didn't negate the rest of his life, which included selling and using drugs in addition to pimping and other crimes. Yet the inner voice to which Jason had begun to listen was clear and steadfast. No matter how far and hard Jason ran after the life of crime, hurting himself and others, that inner voice continued to knock on the door of Jason's heart. The healing was beginning to happen inside him.

Even so, it would take another year before Jason would relinquish his horrific existence. Finally, after one particularly harrowing experience, he did what he had done several times during his destructive and disastrous life of crime. He went back to his one place of stability and security—to his parents who had never quit believing in him even though they had never condoned his sordid lifestyle. Despite the anguish he had caused them, they welcomed their son with open arms, an act that still humbles him.

A Life Reclaimed

Although Jason's struggle to get his life back on track would be studded with pain, he had finally made the decision to live a God-fearing life, no matter the cost. From that day forward, he never returned to the life of crime and destruction.

Jason now speaks to groups of young people, as well as to individuals of all ages. Having seen a lot of perpetrators in my life, and very few who have truly turned their lives around, I am a major skeptic when it comes to believing in real-life change for someone who has devastated so many lives. However, I can testify to Jason's honest turnaround. Today, Jason is my friend. He is happily married, a father, and a man who radiates the love and acceptance of one who has experienced amazing grace, without a hint of religiosity. I can truly vouch for the fact that his is a transformed life.

Miraculous or Supported?

So what is the difference between Jason and so many others whose lives never change? One can never really know the full answer to that question. Jason's parents—who continued to love him unconditionally even though they never condoned, accepted, or tolerated the havoc he wreaked in so many lives—prayed for him without stopping. They asked their many friends (myself included) and family to pray for him over the years as well. "The restoration God has done in my life is unquestionably nothing short of a miracle in and of itself." Whether or not one believes in miracles, this story is one of lasting change.

Jason now helps others who have lived a life of crime find the help they need to turn their lives around. One of the first people Jason helped after getting his life in order recently graduated from our state university with honors and is gainfully employed.

Inside the Game

How is it that pimps operate? How are they able to convince young girls that life with them will be better than life with their parents or life on the street?

It is not happenstance, as you will see in the next few paragraphs. Pimps are deliberate and ruthless in the way they systematically groom and then take possession of their victims, fully intending to sell their human flesh for sheer profit. Narcissistic desires for being in power and looking good take a close second place in these predators' priorities. How are they able to successfully victimize precious and valuable human beings time and again?

Make no mistake; potential victims are prepared for the pimp by our culture. Objectification of women is at an all-time high. Sexualized media is preparing, and some say even grooming, our children for the world of sex trafficking. Music, video games, movies, and television—they all send a message that sexual promiscuity is the norm, that beauty for women equates to being sexy, and that women should be all these things to appeal to a man. Additionally, if a woman can attract a man, it seems to equate to proof in our culture that she is of value.

Never has it been more popular to be famous, and fame is highly valued in our society today. We have noted celebrities such as Paris Hilton and Kim Kardashian whom the media often touts as "famous for being famous." Others who began as child actresses for Disney or Nickelodeon shows have grown up to set new standards in lewd dancing, dressing, and acting.

Celebrities teach our sons they must look and act tough. Even if a guy isn't wearing droopy pants that hang low to reveal underwear and more, what they wear must give off a macho look. Some have not been influenced by hip-hop culture yet have still bought into society's message that girls are to be viewed for purposes of fantasy and lust. In fact, they may believe that is what girls really want. Recently I heard someone say that it was more important in his neighborhood to be tough than to be educated, to be street savvy than to be kind and respectful to women. Being macho also means having females your own age a bit in awe of you and maybe fear you a little. Ordinary slang refers to girls as b–tches, hookers, whores, or hoes. If a guy has a girlfriend, she is often referred to as his "old lady" or "b–tch," sex is an expectation, and he must be the man in the relationship and take charge. Sexting and trying girls out sexually is common, and "friends with benefits" is accepted as normal.

What do celebrities teach our daughters? They teach them how to dress scantily and sexy. And with the airbrushed media, if a young girl doesn't look as good as the airbrushed star, she needs to try harder, get thinner. In fact, nine in ten girls say the fashion industry (89 percent) or the media (88 percent) place a lot of pressure on teen girls to be thin.[3]

Teens often spend hours in front of bathroom mirrors learning how to look sexy in all their selfies and other photos. Boys aren't the only ones who refer to girls as b–tches, hookers, whores, or hoes; teen girls commonly refer to each other using those terms. Being sexual is what everyone is doing, and you should *want* to do it; if not, don't tell anyone you are a virgin or not sexually active. Media teaches teen girls that they should be able to dance using grinding and twerking, and it is understood that the purpose is to turn a man on while dancing. Sex is no big deal, comes with no strings attached, and anyone who makes a big deal out of it needs to get over it.

Being attractive is good, but flawless is better. Being attractive means being thin, maybe too thin, and wearing clothes that barely cover one's underwear, which is optional. After all, that's how the stars dress.

If girls can be attractive enough, everything will fall at their feet and all their heart's desires will come true. They will be loved in a spectacular way, they will have plenty of money, and the fame that will surround them will give them more attention than they can handle. And even if the dream of fame fails, if they are sexy they will at least have boys who want them for sex, which in today's teen culture is a must.

Most of all, being attractive means being sexy. The words *hand-some* and *pretty* have been replaced by the unisex word *sexy*. The word *sex* has gone from being barely spoken in public a couple generations ago to being the word to describe an attractive person.

Recently in my work I saw a photo on a teen's Facebook page of her one-year-old nephew who was dressed up like a gang member. Her caption read, "This is the sexiest man alive." I cringed at the message she had written, both for how her mind was thinking and for how this toddler was being groomed before he could barely walk.

All of this is pre-grooming for sex traffickers who are ready to turn out young girls as "fresh meat" or "barely legal."

Many songs top the billboard charts with titles like "B–tches Ain't S–t," which describes grabbing the "hoes" and grabbing cash; "B–tch Betta Have My Money," which describes keeping "hoes" "on point" and how the pimp expects money; and "One Less B–tch," which describes the murder of "hoes" who do not comply with their pimp.

With the culture our children live in, it is no wonder that when traffickers approach them, they understand one another. The grooming process has already begun before the next step with the trafficker.

Being a parent in our society is tougher than ever before, but one thing is for sure: if our children understand that all people are equal and learn to respect themselves and others as equals, that is the beginning of "ungrooming" what society has inflicted. If we all view ourselves and others as equals, there will be no place for human trafficking—ever.

There's Nothing Cool about Pimps

Jason, the pimp discussed earlier in this chapter, chose his misguided, destructive path because it provided him with the three things he thought might ease his pain: money, power, and respect.

Popular culture in the United States doesn't just condone pimping, it often glamorizes it. In feature movies, on television, and in the world of hard-core hip-hop music, pimping is often presented as a thrilling line of "work" to which young men should proudly aspire. One 2005 hard-core hip-hop song titled "It's Hard Out Here for a Pimp," which chronicles the sometimes violent struggles of a street pimp to make a living off his "b–tches" and "hoes," won an Academy Award for best song.[4]

In too many neighborhoods, pimps are looked up to as symbols of success. Why not? They have all the trappings that money can buy, and their jobs are even celebrated. And not just by the entertainment industry. In a large number of cities, including our own small town, "pimp and ho" parties are publicly advertised and celebrated at local nightclubs.

Excuse me?

There is nothing at all glamorous or socially acceptable about pimps or pimping. Real-life pimps are among the worst kind of predators our culture has to offer, and they pose a very real danger to young women and girls in America today. They are criminals who recruit, coerce, and threaten our young women and girls, then sell them into prostitution. They traffick their victims from brothel to brothel and from town to town, making it extremely difficult, sometimes impossible, for law enforcement or the victims' families to locate them.

Despite their abysmal record, we elevate pimps in modern speech—especially among the young—by using the word *pimp* in a positive context. "Wow! You're pimped out today!" is said to indicate that someone is extremely well dressed. What a way to refer to what was once known as our Sunday best. And what a crime. Common sense tells us that the word *pimp* should at best indicate something ugly and vulgar. Instead, on every episode of the popular MTV (Music Television) program "Pimp

My Ride," technicians, body and paint specialists, and artists convert people's beat-up, barely running wrecks into "pimped out" automobiles that their owners can drive down the street with pride.

Since I have become involved in the movement to stop human trafficking, I have come to see the ugliness of the word *pimp* and all it implies. And although I'm not easily offended, I do take offense at its casual use. Using the word *pimp* in the ways I've listed above—and in similar ways—not only breaks down moral and social barriers to pimping and sex trafficking, it disguises the true ugliness of what real-life pimps do. Its casual use also dehumanizes the women and young girls who fall victim to pimps and puts a glamorous face on the ugliness. Pimps are human traffickers. Pimps are modern slave masters.

We need to debunk this word so that children understand a pimp isn't the ultimate superstar but rather a criminal who rapes, beats, and uses people and destroys lives. If somebody were to tell me, "Wow! You're really pimped out today!" I would answer, "No, I'm not. I haven't raped anybody, and no, I haven't beaten anybody. I haven't kept anybody imprisoned, and I haven't coerced anyone to do the most degrading thing in the world for my own personal profit. No, I'm not pimped out."

Pimps are sometimes considered the worst kind of human traffickers because they use their victims over and over again until they're traded or discarded, or, since few manage to escape, until they die.

To be clear, though I've been using the word *pimp* to refer to sex traffickers, there are a variety of pimps out there. Morally, I see little difference among those profiting off of human slave labor, whether in a factory, a home, a field, or a brothel. They're all selling humans, so they're all slaveholders. I don't know any decent person who wants to celebrate that.

Identifying Human Traffickers in Your Backyard

A reality check in terms of semantics is just the start of what's needed. We must be willing to expose any pimps—any human traffickers—who all too often operate in our very own communities, even posing as upstanding community members.

Human traffickers could be people who are considered virtuous members of your church or community. Think about Given's story in chapter 2 and Pastor Keith who recruited him and others from Zambia. Is there a worse form of depravity than using God's name to abuse others?

Human traffickers could be respectable local businessmen who own secret sweatshops. Remember Quyen Truong? Kil Soo Lee, the man who held her and hundreds of others in his American Samoa factory where he forced them to sew garments, did business with some of this country's top retail clothing brands.

Human traffickers could be restaurateurs in your hometown. How many people enjoyed a meal at the family chain where Charito worked without having a clue that she and the other Asians were being so mistreated?

Human traffickers could be your neighbors, no matter the income level in which you live. Shyima is only one of an untold number of household slaves being held in this country. A 2004 report concludes, "The second highest incidence of forced labor takes place in domestic service in United States homes."[5] And that doesn't even include the countless sex slaves squirreled away in brothels discreetly run out of ordinary homes in perfectly ordinary neighborhoods.

These human traffickers—these low-down, disgusting pimps—excel at three things: manipulation, power, and control. They're well versed in classic brainwashing techniques and take pride in being able to bend other people to their will. A former pimp I interviewed explained that pimps are "at the top of the food chain" because instead of selling dope and setting yourself up to get busted or killed, "you control [your girls] with your mind and get the money without doing anything. You put them at risk and you don't put yourself at risk with jail, all the stuff that can go wrong in that lifestyle."[6]

The pimp world has changed since my source got out of the life of crime, and not for the better. Hard to believe, but life has gotten worse for the victims of pimps. Pimp culture used to encourage pride in the fact that they controlled their girls by psychological control. They played manipulation games and still cruelly treated their victims, but with much less physical brutality and torture than many of today's pimps. However, now we have what is called the "gorilla pimp." Younger pimps have been conditioned to believe that they must take what they want by brute force and torture.

After all, that is what our hip-hop culture teaches: drugs, alcohol, women, and whatever else brings a young man pleasure should be used for his status and gratification. Songs about pimping encourage dominance by the male, disrespect for females, and violence to maintain that dominance. Both pimping and drug dealing are seen as glamorous, and they are intertwined in this world.

Our challenge lies in changing attitudes so that someone who pimps girls is seen as the slave master he is rather than someone who's cool. Once that happens, then maybe we can begin to stem some of this flow. As young people become more aware of the recruiting tactics of human traffickers, those typically targeted to be victims of human trafficking become more informed and less vulnerable.

Ironically, a large percentage of human trafficking victims are tricked into going with traffickers. Of course, the trafficker doesn't tell them the truth. Instead, they say something like, "Come to America. You'll work in a restaurant and make hundreds of dollars a day in tips." That's huge money to a lot of people, and the victim can easily verify that even busboys can earn large tips in the United States. What they don't realize is that when they get here, instead of waiting tables in that restaurant, they may be dancing a strip pole and having sex for money in a room on the side of the club, with the money going to the perpetrator who traffics them.

That's one of the distinct differences between slavery in the old days and modern slavery. Historically, slaves were captured. Today, most slaves have consented to work for their traffickers. They've just consented to something very different from what they end up in, so they've been duped by someone smart enough, charming enough, and narcissistic enough to pull off a continued series of hoaxes that destroy people's lives. And because the perpetrators lack compassion and see life as being all about them, they see no reason not to lie if it makes them money. In the traffickers' minds, hurting someone is justifiable as long as it pads their own pockets.

The bottom line is that a perpetrator is a perpetrator is a perpetrator, whether he's trafficking slaves for farm work, domestic work, sex, or anything else. Perpetrators do what they do because they profit from it financially and egotistically. It doesn't matter to them that the profit comes at the expense of another.

The very few perpetrators with even a shred of conscience do everything they can to expunge that sense of right and wrong. When Jason Foster devastated his girlfriend Claire's life and the lives of so many others by turning them out, he refused to let himself consider why a girl would "go sell her body, do the most extreme thing in the world and give you all the money and stay with you." He advised a younger pimp he'd taken under his wing to never even consider why someone would be willing to do that. "If you sit here and try to ponder that and think about it, you will go crazy, because there is absolutely no sane reason," he told him.[7] In short, he knew what he was doing was immoral. At the time, however, that just didn't matter.

For traffickers, the horrific cost to their victims isn't even a consideration. The sex slaves, the factory workers and farmworkers, the domestic or restaurant workers are simply a tool to make the perpetrator money—and in the process to make him look important. To a perpetrator, using a victim is as casual and calculated as a construction worker picking up a hammer.

So how do you recognize a human trafficker? You can't tell just by looking, the same way you can't tell whether someone batters his wife just by looking at him. How do you recognize abusers? They abuse. How do you recognize traffickers? They traffick. There is nothing glamorous about a pimp or any other kind of human trafficker. And unless we see them committing the crime, we often cannot recognize them.

But that doesn't mean that there isn't hope for some of these people, no matter how far they've fallen. As we saw in Jason's story, with intervention and a deep desire to reform, some can be redeemed. However, that does not negate the necessity for prosecution and for restitution to their victims.

I have met many people who want to find traffickers and punish them in the same way they have tortured their victims. While I can understand how one might feel that way, especially if the victim was their child, those acts will serve no good purpose.

Occasionally I encounter those who want to stand up for the perpetrators because they are people too. My response is that I absolutely believe perpetrators are humans with rights and should be afforded dignity and opportunity to reform, and I hope they find all the help and direction they need behind bars.

What can we do? We can help those whose children are missing by reposting information about missing children on the internet once we have verified that they are still missing. We can join search and rescue groups that do incredible work in locating missing children. We can help put up posters and encourage someone whose child or loved one is missing.

But we can never lose sight of who is the perpetrator and who is the victim. The crimes they have committed are some of the worst on earth. Some of their victims never recover. Some will commit suicide because the pain of survival is too much for them. Human trafficking laws must be improved, services must be improved. In the meantime, those of us who are in this fight must do all we can from day to day to help raise awareness about human trafficking. This is a messy world in which we live, and we must never lose sight of the goal to stop human trafficking that is detrimental to all.

For Discussion

1. Has your view of the life of a pimp changed since reading this book? If so, how? How might those changes be reflected in your life?

2. Pimps are not the only types of perpetrators of human trafficking. Discuss several types of traffickers and how they might be similar or different.

3. If Jason Foster could be redeemed, certainly there are others who can also find their way out of the life of inflicting pain and the crime of human trafficking. Many, however, never change. Why do you think Jason's life changed but many others do not?

4. Money and power seem to be the most common motivators for traffickers. How can we use the power of our spending to help stop modern slavery?

5. Locate a news story about a trafficker. Discuss what might have been his or her motivation for the crime and how we might make it hard to be a trafficker in our community.

10

On the Front Lines
of Modern Slavery

Love begins at home, and it is not how much we do, but how
much love we put in that action.

—Mother Teresa

The problem of human trafficking can seem as overwhelming as it is
grim. But there are those who are working to change this situation,
some in paid positions and some volunteering their time and even
their own money. Each one brings something incredibly valuable
to this fight. In this last chapter, I want to share some stories of
hope and courage, stories of those who have chosen to transform
small ideas to actions that are making a big difference.

Protecting Communities against Slavery

In November 2008, during my trip to India, I learned that some villages that had been completely enslaved prior to the intervention of nongovernmental organizations (NGOs) had not only been freed, but had actually been effectively protected against future trafficking.

In this village-by-village antislavery operation, first schools are formed and children are educated. Then antislavery activists begin to work with the women in the community, followed by the men. Once the women and men are on board—with a new understanding about what slavery is and that citizens have rights, and possibly even recognizing they had been enslaved—the villagers begin to come together as a community. They have meetings to discuss slavery, as well as what to do if the traffickers come and how to protect one another from trafficking.

At some point, the village becomes immune to human trafficking. The community awareness and determination to keep slavery out makes it undesirable for traffickers, especially since the chance of them succeeding in their criminal activities in the midst of all the awareness is low and they face the possibility of prosecution. So, as one local declared, "The traffickers don't come here anymore." We can with confidence label that village *slave-proofed*.

We can wage a similar campaign here in America. When the level of awareness becomes so high that entire communities stand together against trafficking, that is the beginning of being slave-proofed. At that point, safety and services are provided to help those who have been trafficked and to prevent others from being trafficked. Law enforcement and prosecutors successfully prosecute traffickers to the full extent of the law. When these things happen, it makes that place undesirable for traffickers, so they leave the region to go where trafficking is more profitable. I like to say, at that point, those communities have made it hard to be a trafficker. In everything I do, I want to make it hard to be a trafficker!

We have begun that process in the community where I live, and the entire area is starting to become aware. Once people realize that slavery exists here in the United States and that it's in our communities, I find that people *want* to be on board. They want to help fight slavery. Tips about possible trafficking activities begin to flow in. Law enforcement officers follow up on those reports, once they too become more aware, and work to stop this crime.

Change like this, however, does not happen overnight. There have been times when I have worked successfully with an entire agency for years, only to have the leadership change and the new leadership be busy with other priorities besides anti-trafficking efforts. It takes time, patience, consistent work, and the ability to bite your tongue when someone doesn't accept your message. Sometimes when a door closes, it takes time and many efforts to coax that door open again. This is a battle where we often take two steps forward and one or two steps back. The point is that we must keep trying because the lives of children and others in our communities depend on it.

It is a very uncomfortable self-assessment as we begin to understand our part in this—how we unknowingly participate or react when we see human trafficking. It's more comfortable to try to keep that "slavery dust" from getting on us instead of getting involved, says Lou de Baca, US Ambassador-at-Large, Office to Monitor and Combat Trafficking in Persons.[1] But if we all link arms, putting aside different political or religious beliefs, and join together in the shared hope of stopping modern slavery in our lifetime, we can win this immensely important fight.

Many people are doing tremendous things. In law enforcement, one of those stars is Keith Bickford.

Keith is a big guy with a big heart. He's a Multnomah County deputy sheriff and a deputized Special US Marshal charged with investigating and bringing justice to cases of human trafficking throughout the state of Oregon. He's also the founder and leader of Oregonians against Trafficking Humans, the same organization for which I lead the Central Oregon contingency.

However, there's more to the man than his credentials. Some people do their jobs and do them well. Bickford certainly does his best to bring justice to human traffickers to the fullest extent of the law. But he goes beyond that. He cares so deeply about stopping human trafficking that it's as though his heart beats to do the work. He does everything within his power and within the law to rescue victims and sees to it that they receive services to which they're entitled.

When I asked Keith about his greatest victories, he pointed to a case where a victim was freed from the horrific farm labor slavery in which he was trapped. He received the surgeries, follow-up medical care, and counseling he needed to recover from the damage his captors had inflicted on him. The perpetrators, however, were never charged or convicted. "To me, that doesn't seem like a very big win," Bickford says. "But every time I see the victim, he thanks me for saving his life, so I guess that's okay. I'll take it."[2]

Bickford not only helps human trafficking victims directly, he helps them by sharing his expertise with other agencies. When I was contacted to help our first trafficking victim in Bend, Oregon, we contacted Bickford. He gave us numbers to call for services to help her, tips about pitfalls we might encounter in the process, and the correct connections for law enforcement and legal counsel. In short, he patiently and carefully walked us through every step along the way. Each day when I called, he inquired about how the victim was doing. Even though he had never met her, he obviously cared about her as a person.

Bickford doesn't just devote his energies to fighting trafficking one perpetrator—or one victim—at a time. He also trains and engages law enforcement and community agencies, and he has done a tremendous amount of work to help make the dream of more shelter beds for underage sex-trafficking victims available. I've often said that Bickford's biggest risk is that his heart is as big as all outdoors. He is a man whose life is like a rock dropping in the water, with all the ripples representing many saved lives and many new forces engaged in the fight against human trafficking.

But we can't rely on just law enforcement, government, social services, and large nonprofits. Shortly after I began doing anti–human trafficking work, my friend Sherry, who lives in a city six hours away, contacted me. She had just read my book and was deeply saddened to learn about the extent of human trafficking here in our country. She was aghast at her newfound knowledge. "If I was so unaware that this is happening everywhere, then so are many other Americans." As she began making suggestions to raise awareness, I asked her if she would be willing to help by doing that in my organization, In Our Backyard. Sherry didn't feel like she had the knowledge to contribute as much as she would like, but she had a willing heart. She has an especially tender heart and didn't feel that she could work on the front lines as I do, but she would do what she could to support my work.

I had known Sherry for thirty years at that point and knew she was smart and had deep character and that if she committed to something, she would do it well. I also knew she had excellent professional experience, having recently retired as a vice president program and project manager of a large bank. I knew that even from six hours away, she could effectively do administrative work.

She accepted the challenge, and that was five years ago. Today, she is an invaluable asset to my work. I often think I couldn't do all the things I do without her. Not only is she doing executive-level administration, but she is a confidante, a sounding board, and someone who does organizational tasks for me that are far beyond my capabilities. Sherry has never had to experience the front lines, but she makes a big difference on those front lines across the nation as she works on her computer and phone at home. Sherry is also one of my heroes.

In the end, it's up to us as individuals to challenge this heinous crime taking place in our backyards. We can each invest our talents and life circumstances to join the fight. While the work can be difficult at times, when we see progress and life-saving opportunities, it is worth every late night and every challenging moment. I often say, "If it was my child who was out there, I'd want others doing everything they could to help her." Every victim or potential victim is someone's daughter, son, brother, sister, friend, or loved one. They deserve our help.

We have made great progress. Before the year 2000, human trafficking wasn't even a crime in the United States. These crimes were prosecuted under other statutes, such as forced prostitution or indentured servitude. The Trafficking Victims Protection Act of 2000 has been updated multiple times, and state laws are constantly improving.

When I first began studying and doing human trafficking work in 2006, if I mentioned the words "human trafficking," the majority of people did not even understand the meaning of that term. Today, Americans have woken up to not only know what human trafficking is, but to the reality that human trafficking is not just something that happens in other countries. People know it happens here and are beginning to do something about it.

Evidence of this comes from the National Human Trafficking Hotline, which reports that between 2008 and 2012 calls to the hotline increased 259 percent. Between 2007 and 2012 they responded to 5,932 cases of sex trafficking and 2,027 cases of labor trafficking.[3]

Thousands of anti–human trafficking organizations have been formed across America. Even in small jurisdictions, most law enforcement and prosecutors have a designated person whose caseload includes human trafficking cases. Midsize to large cities generally have multiple salaried positions designated for anti–human trafficking work.

Prevention is a huge part of this work. Having spent time with many survivors, I always come away saying that I would much rather have prevented the trafficking and torture from ever happening in the first place than seeing what victims have to go through to find healing and peace.

We have made progress, and if you have been working to raise awareness, you are a part of that progress. Many have been rescued from lives of pain and torture, and many more prevented from ever falling into this horrible atrocity.

The question I am most often asked is, "What can I do to help stop trafficking?" Although I have written numerous ideas in this book, I would like to answer that question with one final, remarkable story.

Lyn Thompson[4], the mother of four beautiful grown daughters, had a passion for justice. In 2007 she and her daughters learned about modern slavery by reading a book titled *Not for Sale*. They are a family who puts actions behind their outrage, so Lyn, her four daughters, and another friend had a conference call, stretching across the nation in different states to determine, "What shall we do?"

Sometimes we must come up with audacious goals to get things done. By the end of their call, they had certainly done that. Kylla Lanier, one of Thompson's daughters, told me, "We decided that our mission would be to end human exploitation worldwide." Seriously.

Their next step was to turn their good intentions into concrete action. Two of the women cofounded an anti–human trafficking coalition in Oklahoma, and another put together a human trafficking awareness conference in Denver involving many of the major anti-trafficking nonprofits.

It was during one of those breakout sessions at that October 2008 conference that Kylla heard something that seemed large but doable. The trainer, Phil Gazley, said he was trying to organize gas station workers and attendants to be aware of trafficking and to know how to be part of the solution.

Later, as she met with her family and others who were involved in their new endeavor, Lyn told about growing up as the daughter of motel owners in El Paso, Texas. She remembered many of their clients were truckers whom Lyn remembered as nice guys. "If you got the truckers looking out for victims and trained them on the signs of potential trafficking and empowered them with a response, that would be a big help." That idea is what launched what is now often referred to as TAT—Truckers Against Trafficking.

Although they initially knew no one in the trucking business, didn't know the lingo, and didn't really know the industry, they searched until they found someone who could help them navigate this new territory. They spent the next season learning about the trucking industry, learning more about human trafficking, and getting their mission statement out there about how they wanted to help.

Funding is a major issue for nearly every nonprofit, but they each saved their money and contributed to the work as they could to help the success of their new nonprofit. After all, if they were going to end human exploitation, it would cost everyone, and they were willing to start with their own pocketbooks. They began looking for opportunities to educate the trucking industry about human trafficking and about how each trucker could be a part of the solution to stop trafficking and find help for victims.

Not only did it cost these courageous and committed founders money to start this organization, but it also cost a tremendous amount of time, including lost sleep and giving up other things they used to enjoy. When I asked about the costs, Kylla, who is now TAT's deputy director, noted, "It even costs you a little bit of your heart." She explained that if people get stuck in sympathy they can crash and burn. But if that sympathy is converted to empathy, which moves a person's pain, anger, sadness, and rage into action at the injustice of it all, then it can truly help stop trafficking. "You can read something or watch something and do nothing, but you've got to move it to the next stage and do something."

After partnering with the anti-trafficking organization iEmpathize, which combats human trafficking through arts and media, TAT's training video was produced. The video opened many doors for TAT within the trucking industry as industry executives and truckers alike were moved to action after watching it.

When executives of the national travel plaza chain TA/Petro watched the video, they immediately initiated TAT training for thousands of their employees. They have continued to partner with TAT in the fight against human trafficking by sending their general managers to TAT's coalition-building conferences, which bring together law enforcement and members of the trucking industry for a half day of training to further close loopholes to traffickers.

Likewise, the Ryder trucking company implemented TAT training for all twenty-four thousand of their employees. They also promote TAT at their events and use their influence within the trucking industry to raise awareness and encourage other businesses to train their employees and contribute to TAT's cause.

Kendis Paris, TAT's executive director, notes, "Human trafficking happens at every level of society. You see it in a myriad of venues and industries. It is notable how the trucking industry has refused to turn a blind eye to this crime, and has taken a strong stand against it."

And the proof of the trucking industry's embracing of TAT's mission is evident in the number of calls to the National Human Trafficking Resource Center (NHTRC) hotline. In 2007 when the NHTRC began, they received three calls from truckers. In 2013, they received over three hundred calls from truckers. In 2014 the number has continued to grow. Nicole Moler, director of the NHTRC, said,

> Truckers are now one of the most motivated and well-organized industry groups working on this issue, and their reports have led to countless arrests and recoveries of victims across the country. TAT has been instrumental in creating a community of activists who are speaking out against human trafficking and directly impacting the lives of victims. TAT is a leader in the fight against human trafficking, and we regularly cite their work as an example for other industries to follow. I have no doubt that their work has and will continue to transform our ability to fight human trafficking, and we are proud to partner with them in their efforts to eliminate human trafficking and modern-day slavery.[5]

One such success story comes from TAT's first Harriet Tubman Award recipient, Tracy Mullins. Tracy is a general manager of the Petro Stopping Center in Spokane, Washington. She is a Spokane resident and a fourteen-year veteran of the transportation industry. She credits the TAT training required of all employees/managers of TravelCenters of America with playing a pivotal role in her awareness of "something that could be wrong."

In relating the incident that earned her the award, Tracy recounted that she was walking into a restaurant near her travel plaza to talk to the manager. She noticed two young girls sitting with an older man. "Not that the situation was odd," she said, "but the man looked as if something could be wrong. I positioned myself close enough to the table to hear the young girls ask for a ride to Seattle. At this point, the images of all the young girls from the training video were going through my mind." She approached the table and asked the girls if everything was okay. "One of the girls told me the man was her uncle. The man seemed very uncomfortable and removed himself from the situation. The young girls then asked other drivers for a ride."

Tracy realized there was a problem and notified law enforcement. The girls turned out to be runaways from a neighboring state with only five dollars between them. She stated, "This is a very special award for me, because, as a mother, I know we helped two young girls not become a statistic that day."

There were challenges, as there are with any endeavor at any level of society, but TAT has stuck to their mission to educate, equip, empower, and mobilize the trucking industry to recognize the signs of human trafficking and combat it. TAT's social media platform has been a great conduit for honest conversations and dialogue on more controversial issues surrounding the anti-trafficking message.

"It has been really rewarding seeing the trucking industry's depth of understanding develop on the issue of human trafficking. As so many truckers have stated on our Facebook page or through tweets, they don't care what gender, race, age, or nationality a victim is; if they are a victim, they want them recovered and helped. It is thrilling to see drivers educating fellow drivers about the truths of prostitution, pornography, and how they intertwine with human trafficking," Kylla shared.

She hears of truckers who once believed the women in prostitution were criminals, but now buy them a cup of coffee, give potential victims a TAT wallet card, and tell them there is hope. They treat them with compassion and respect, telling them there are "people who will care about you and help you out of this life if you ever want out." Survivors have told TAT they wish such aware truckers had been out there when they were being trafficked and have pledged to help TAT in any way they can.

TAT's founders suggest that people who want to assist in this fight against trafficking learn and keep learning so they have a complete analysis of the problem and can seek viable solutions. Along with that, people should look for opportunities to help an already existing nonprofit according to their own personality, skill set, and time. As one learns more about human trafficking, areas of tremendous need are uncovered, which then offers the opportunity to begin to step out into meeting those needs. TAT would love to see nationwide efforts to partner with the taxi, bus, train, and shipping industries. "If groups could take on one segment of the transportation industry, learn about it, and fully engage them in the fight against human trafficking, we could cripple many networks and modes of transportation that traffickers use to exploit their victims. We would *love* to see that happen," Kylla said.

Actions Speak Louder Than Words

In the end, it is about putting action behind the emotions and the talk. The trucking industry and TAT have done just that. TAT has begun to see changes in the trucking industry's culture around the issue of trafficking and prostitution. What originally seemed like an audacious mission has made a huge difference. TAT and truckers are making it difficult to be a trafficker in places that traffickers once viewed as lucrative.

This wonderfully daring group of courageous and hardworking women has made a huge difference by making trafficking at truck stops much more difficult for perpetrators. Indeed, they are heroes in the anti-trafficking movement, and TAT's work is a shining example of engaging an industry as a partner in this fight against human trafficking. Well done, TAT!

There are many things I like about TAT's story. First, they didn't lose sight of the prize they were seeking—justice. They all chipped in with money and hard work, both on the days they felt like it and on the days they didn't, and they kept going. They weren't afraid to dream big, and they kept marching forward even when the naysayers said it couldn't or shouldn't be done. They have linked arms with other abolitionist groups with similar hearts. But fundamentally, the thing I like about TAT's story is that they were practical enough to find one industry, learn that industry, embrace that industry, and link arms with them to stop trafficking.

Since this is the last chapter in this book, I suspect you may be asking yourself what you personally can do to stop human trafficking. If you are up for something big, it will cost you time, money, sleep, and maybe more. (I know, the glamour in this idea just exited.) Might I suggest thinking of an industry you are familiar with that could make a difference in anti-trafficking? One idea might be beauty salons. Sex-trafficking victims are often "treated" to having their nails or hair done or are taken to tanning salons. Other industries might be hotels/motels, restaurants, shoe stores, convenience stores, and other retail businesses. For labor trafficking, one might target canneries, wineries, hotels/motels, housekeeping services, real estate or rental companies, plumbers, electricians, and mail or package carriers. While not all of these industries are trafficking humans, they may come in contact with other businesses or make business calls at homes where they might spot victims.

Truly, the list is endless. Ordinary citizens can find themselves in contact with victims of human trafficking anyplace a victim could be performing labor trafficking, such as restaurants, farming, or even in our neighborhoods. Sex-trafficked individuals are taken by their traffickers to hotels, restaurants, gas stations, and any number of places. Individuals or entire industries can be responsible for the saving of many lives, as the trucking industry has been and continues to be.

The fight to free about 27 million people living in slavery[6]—from nearly every nation and territory on earth—seems like a truly impossible task. Even the notion of freeing the hundreds of thousands of trafficked individuals in this country seems unattainable. But as you have read this book, you have seen that people are making a difference. I see part of our job as anti-trafficking activists as making it hard to be a trafficker. Together we can do this.

If awareness is raised and industries are united against trafficking; if children are aware and tell someone responsible when they are approached; if the nation becomes so aware that we designate dollars for services for runaways so they don't feel their only option is to get help from a trafficker; if the nation becomes so aware that we designate dollars for professional and loving shelters for both minors and adult survivors; if we all speak up at every opportunity instead of turning a deaf ear—we can do this.

The old adage "How do you eat an elephant?" is true in this movement: One. Bite. At. A. Time. One compassionate phone call, one poster hung, one loving conversation at a time. We can stop human trafficking in our backyard in our lifetime.

For Discussion

1. How has this book changed your understanding of human trafficking or modern slavery in the United States?

2. Is there some industry you feel you could target or some way you think you might be able to help stop slavery in our world today?

3. In reading about some of the ways others have worked to stop slavery, have you been inspired? If so, how?

4. If what you've learned about human trafficking has been valuable to you, can you identify a friend to whom you might recommend this book?

Appendix

Recognizing the Signs

Red Flags and Possible Indicators of Human Trafficking

The Polaris Project[1]

Are you or someone you know being trafficked? Is trafficking happening in your community? Is the situation you encountered human trafficking? The following is a list of potential red flags and indicators of human trafficking. If you see any of these red flags, call the National Human Trafficking Hotline at 1-888-373-7888 or text "HELP" to BeFree (233733) immediately to report the situation.

Common Work and Living Conditions

The Individual(s) in Question:

- Is not free to leave or come and go as he/she wishes
- Is under 18 and is providing commercial sex acts

- Is in the commercial sex industry and has a pimp/manager
- Is unpaid, paid very little, or paid only through tips
- Works excessively long and/or unusual hours
- Is not allowed breaks or suffers under unusual restrictions at work
- Owes a large debt and is unable to pay it off
- Was recruited through false promises concerning the nature and conditions of his/her work
- High security measures exist in the work and/or living locations (e.g., opaque windows, boarded-up windows, bars on windows, barbed wire, security cameras, etc.)

Poor Mental Health or Abnormal Behavior

- Is fearful, anxious, depressed, submissive, tense, or exhibits nervous/paranoid behavior
- Exhibits unusually fearful or anxious behavior after law enforcement is brought up
- Avoids eye contact

Poor Physical Health

- Lacks health care
- Appears malnourished
- Shows signs of physical and/or sexual abuse, physical restraint, confinement, or torture

Lack of Control

- Has few or no personal possessions
- Is not in control of his/her own money; has no financial records or bank account

- Is not in control of his/her own identification documents (ID or passport)
- Is not allowed or able to speak for himself/herself (a third party may insist on being present and/or translating)

Other

- Claims of just visiting and inability to clarify where he/she is staying/address
- Lack of knowledge of whereabouts and/or does not know what city he/she is in
- Loss of sense of time
- Has numerous inconsistencies in his/her story

Note: This list is not exhaustive and rather represents a selection of possible indicators. Also, the red flags in this list may not be present in all trafficking cases and are not cumulative.

Notes

Chapter 1 Modern Slavery

1. Testimony of Ernie Allen, president and CEO of the National Center for Missing and Exploited Children, "Domestic Minor Sex Trafficking," hearing of the US House of Representatives Committee on the Judiciary Subcommittee on Crime, Terrorism and Homeland Security, September 15, 2010, http://www.gpo.gov/fdsys/pkg/CHRG-111hhrg58250/html/CHRG-111hhrg58250.htm.

2. "Teen Girls' Stories of Sex Trafficking in U.S.," ABC News *Primetime*, February 9, 2006, http://abcnews.go.com/Primetime/story?id=1596778&page=1.

3. Kevin Bales, *Disposable People* (Berkeley: University of California Press, 1999), 8.

4. US Department of Health and Human Services, "HHS Fights to Stem Human Trafficking," news release, August 15, 2006, http://www.hhs.gov/news/factsheet/humantrafficking.html.

5. US Department of State, "Trafficking in Persons Report," June 2005, http://www.state.gov/documents/organization/47255.pdf.

6. "Assessment of U.S. Activities to Combat Trafficking in Persons," June 2004, http://www.justice.gov/archive/ag/annualreports/tr2004/us_assessment_2004.pdf.

7. Heather J. Clawson, Nicole Dutch, Amy Solomon, and Lisa Goldblatt Grace, "Human Trafficking Into and Within the United States: A Review of the Literature," US Department of Health and Human Services, August 2009, http://aspe.hhs.gov/hsp/07/humantrafficking/litrev/.

8. Ibid.

9. Trafficking Victims Protection Act, http://www.state.gov/documents/organization/226850.pdf.

10. US Department of State, "Trafficking in Persons Report," June 2004, http://www.state.gov/documents/organization/34158.pdf.

11. Linda A. Smith, Taryn Rachel Mastrean, and Samantha Healy Vardaman, "Domestic Minor Sex Trafficking: Child Sex Slavery in Arizona," Shared Hope

International, December 2010, http://sharedhope.org/wp-content/uploads/2012/09/ArizonaRA.pdf. See also J. Greene, S. Ennett, and C. Ringwalt, "Prevalence and Correlates of Survival Sex among Runaway and Homeless Youth," *American Journal of Public Health* 89, no. 9 (1999): 1406.

12. Connecticut Department of Children and Families, "A Child Welfare Response to Domestic Minor Sex Trafficking," n.d., http://www.ct.gov/dcf/lib/dcf/humantrafficing/pdf/response_to_domestic_minot_sex_trafficking.pdf.

13. US Department of Homeland Security Blue Campaign, "Human Trafficking 101 for School Administrators and Staff," http://www.dhs.gov/sites/default/files/publications/blue-campaign/Blue%20Campaign%20-%20Human%20Trafficking%20101%20for%20School%20Administrators%20and%20Staff.pdf.

14. Memorandum by Christopher Carey and Lena Teplitsky, "Commercial Sexual Exploitation of Children (CSEC) in the Portland Metro Area," August 5, 2013, http://www.justice.gov/usao/or/downloads/the_csec_report.pdf.

15. Ibid.

16. Heather J. Clawson et al, "What Is Human Trafficking?" in "Human Trafficking Into and Within the United States," http://aspe.hhs.gov/hsp/07/human trafficking/litrev/#What.

17. Email from Lauran Bethell, December 16, 2014. Used by permission.

18. "Forensic Traumatologist Goes High Tech to Fight Trafficking and Torture," *Technorazzi Magazine*, June 17, 2014, http://technorazzi.com/forensic-trauma tologist-goes-high-tech-to-fight-trafficking/.

19. Minnesota Indian Women's Resource Center, "Early Intervention to Avoid Sex Trading and Trafficking of Minnesota's Female Youth: A Benefit-Cost Analysis" (2012), http://www.castla.org/templates/files/miwrc-benefit-cost-study-summary.pdf.

20. "Key Facts," National Center for Missing & Exploited Children, http://www.missingkids.com/KeyFacts.

21. Marc Klaas, interview with the author, February 3, 2009.

22. Allen testimony, "Domestic Minor Sex Trafficking."

23. National Coalition Against Domestic Violence, "Human Trafficking Facts," August 2006, http://www.ncadv.org/files/HumanTrafficking.pdf.

24. Kevin Bales and Ron Soodalter, *The Slave Next Door* (Berkeley: University of California Press, 2009), 6.

25. Anonymous interview with the author, October 2010.

26. Anonymous interview with the author, October 2010.

27. Sara Jean Green, "McKenna, AGs Confront Backpage.com on Prostitution Ads," *Seattle Times*, September 2, 2011, http://seattletimes.com/text/2016066045.html.

Chapter 2 Eyes That See, Hearts That Care, Hands That Help

1. Given's story has been compiled from personal interviews and emails, which are used by permission of Given Kachepa and Sandy Shepherd. His story is also told in Q. L. Pearce, *Given Kachepa: Advocate for Human Trafficking Victims*, Young Heroes series (Farmington Hills, MI: Kidhaven Press, 2007).

2. DVD of Skype interview with Jesse Arnold and Given Kachepa, Crawford High School, San Diego, CA, August 12, 2014.

3. Ibid.

4. Ibid.

5. Ibid.

6. Ibid.

7. Dunbar Rowland, *Jefferson Davis, Constitutionalist: His Letters, Papers and Speeches* (J. J. Little & Ives Company, 1923), 286.

8. "Rev. Dr. Richard Furman's Exposition of the Views of the Baptists, Relative to the Coloured Population in the United States in a Communication to the Governor of South-Carolina," 2nd ed. (Charleston, SC, 1838). Transcribed by T. Lloyd Benson from the original text in the South Carolina Baptist Historical Collection, Furman University, Greenville, South Carolina. Online at http://eweb .furman.edu/~benson/docs/rcd-fmn1.htm.

9. Global Forum on Human Trafficking, attended by the author, Carlsbad, CA, October 8, 2009.

10. "Harriet Tubman," *Africans in America*, part 4, "Judgment Day," resource bank, *PBS Online*, http://www.pbs.org/wgbh/aia/part4/4p1535.html.

11. Sarah H. Bradford, *Harriet: The Moses of Her People*, (New York: Lockwood & Son, 1886), electronic edition, 15, http://docsouth.unc.edu/neh/harriet /harriet.html.

12. The Freeman Institute Black History Collection, http://www.freemanins titute.com/Tubman.htm.

13. Dan Graves, "Harriet Tubman," Christianity.com, http://www.christian historytimeline.com/GLIMPSEF/Glimpses/glmps130.shtml.

14. Ibid.

15. Ibid.

16. "Harriet Tubman," *PBS Online*, http://www.pbs.org/wgbh/aia/part4/4p1535 .html.

17. http://www.christianhistorytimeline.com/GLIMPSEF/Glimpses/glmps130 .shtml.

18. Bradford, *Harriet*, 61.

19. Ibid.

20. Quoted in Jean M. Humez, *Harriet Tubman: The Life and the Life Stories* (Madison, WI: University of Wisconsin Press, 2003), 151–2.

Chapter 3 From Farm to Factory

1. Malia Zimmerman, "Celebrating Freedom: Justice Finally Achieved for Victims of Human Trafficking in American-Samoa Garment Factory Case," July 3, 2005, Vietnamese Professionals Society website, http://www.vps.org/namcali/gala 2005/news_celebratingfreedom.html.

2. Debra Barayuga, "Victims Call Factory 'Slavery,'" *Honolulu Star-Bulletin News*, July 3, 2005, http://archives.starbulletin.com/2005/07/03/news/story1.html.

3. Zimmerman, "Celebrating Freedom."http://www.vps.org/namcali/gala2005 /news_celebratingfreedom.html.

4. Barayuga, "Victims Call Factory 'Slavery.'"

5. "Slave Wages" (reprinted from the January 27, 2007, *Wall Street Journal*), *Hawaii Reporter*, December 22, 2010, http://www.hawaiireporter.com/slave-wages-from-the-saturday-january-27-2007-wall-street-journal.

6. "Made in the USA?" Institute for Global Labour and Human Rights, February 13, 2001, http://www.globallabourrights.org/reports/made-in-the-u-s-a.

7. Zimmerman, "Celebrating Freedom."

8. Ibid.

9. Barayuga, "Victims Call Factory 'Slavery.'"

10. *United States v. Kil Soo Lee*, 472 F.3d 638 (9th Cir. 2006), http://cases.justia.com/us-court-of-appeals/F3/472/638/473342/.

11. Federal Bureau of Investigation, "Anatomy of an International Human Trafficking Case, Pt. 1," July 16, 2004, http://www.fbi.gov/news/stories/2004/july/kilsoolee_071604.

12. Linda M. Woolf, "Women and Sweatshops," http://www.webster.edu/~woolflm/sweatshops.html.

13. Barayuga, "Victims Call Factory 'Slavery.'"

14. Ibid.

15. http://www.justice.gov/crt/about/app/briefs/lee.pdf.

16. FBI, "Anatomy of an International Human Trafficking Case."

17. "Made in the USA?" The National Labor Committee, February 13, 2001, http://www.globallabourrights.org/reports/made-in-the-u-s-a.

18. Barayuga, "Victims Call Factory 'Slavery.'"

19. FBI, "Anatomy of an International Human Trafficking Case."

20. *US v. Kil Soo Lee*, No. 05-10478, 2006 US App. (9th Cir. May 31, 2006), http://www.justice.gov/crt/about/app/briefs/lee.pdf.

21. US Department of Justice, "Garment Factory Owner Convicted in Largest Ever Human Trafficking Case Prosecuted by the Department of Justice," February 21, 2003, http://www.justice.gov/archive/opa/pr/2003/February/03_crt_108.htm.

22. Ramin Pejan, "Laogai: 'Reform through Labor' in China," *Human Rights Brief: A Legal Resource for the International Human Rights Community* 7, no. 2 (winter 2000), http://www.wcl.american.edu/hrbrief/v7i2/laogai.htm.

23. Ibid.

24. Madison Park, "China Eases One-Child Policy, Ends Education through Labor Camps," CNN World, December 28, 2013, http://www.cnn.com/2013/12/28/world/asia/china-one-child-policy-official/.

25. Kate McGeown, "China's Christians Suffer for Their Faith," BBC News, November 9, 2004, http://news.bbc.co.uk/2/hi/asia-pacific/3993857.stm.

26. Pejan, "Laogai."

27. David Batstone, *Not for Sale* (New York: HarperCollins, 2007), 237.

28. Bales and Soodalter, *The Slave Next Door*, 51.

29. Ronnie Greene, "A Crop of Abuse," *Miami Herald*, September 1, 2003, http://www.miamiherald.com/2003/09/01/56983/a-crop-of-abuse.html.

30. Bales and Soodalter, *The Slave Next Door*, 49.

31. Ibid.

32. Ibid.

33. Ibid.

34. Ibid.

35. Ibid.
36. Greene, "A Crop of Abuse."
37. Ibid.
38. Bales and Soodalter, *The Slave Next Door*, 49.
39. "Dying to Leave," *Wide Angle* special, PBS, 2003.
40. Greene, "A Crop of Abuse."
41. Ibid.
42. Ibid.
43. Bales and Soodalter, *The Slave Next Door*, 49.
44. Ibid., 50.
45. Ibid.
46. Ronnie Greene, "Brutal Farm Labor Bosses Punished, but Not Growers Who Hire Them," *Miami Herald*, September 1, 2003, http://www.latinamericanstudies.org/immigration/farmhands-bosses.htm.
47. Bales and Soodalter, *The Slave Next Door*, 50.
48. Ibid.
49. Ronnie Greene, "Brutal Farm Labor Bosses Punished, but Not Growers Who Hire Them," http://www.fachc.org/pdf/mig_Brutal%20farm%20labor%20bosses%20punished,%20but%20not%20growers%20who%20hire%20them.pdf.
50. Greene, "A Crop of Abuse."
51. Ibid.
52. Ibid.
53. Ibid.
54. Ibid.
55. Ibid.
56. "What Is Fair Trade?" Fair Trade USA, 2015, http://fairtradeusa.org/what-is-fair-trade.

Chapter 4 Just the Help

1. Associated Press, "Child 'Slavery' Now Being Imported to U.S.," NBCNews.com, December 29, 2008, www.msnbc.msn.com/id/28415693/ns/us_news-life/.
2. Mary A. Fischer, "The Slave in the Garage," *Reader's Digest*, May 2008, http://www.rd.com/your-america-inspiring-people-and-stories/slave-in-the-garage/article55737.html.
3. Ibid.
4. AP, "Child 'Slavery' Now Being Imported."
5. Rukmini Callimachi, "Child Maid Trafficking Spreads from Africa to US," *Truthout*, December 29, 2008, http://www.truth-out.org/1229080.
6. Fischer, "The Slave in the Garage."
7. Ibid.
8. Rukmini Callimachi, "Shyima's Story: Now a Teen, a Former Slave Copes with Her Past," January 2, 2009, http://www.heraldnet.com/article/20090102/NEWS02/701029924.
9. Ibid.
10. See Johnny Dodd, "Shyima Hall: My Escape from Slavery," *People* 81, no. 8 (Feb. 24, 2014), http://www.people.com/people/archive/article/0,,20789118,00.html.

11. Yvette Cabrera, "Child Trafficking Victim Speaks Out," *Orange County Register*, September 14, 2009, http://www.ocregister.com/articles/hall-211109-trafficking-pertierra.html?pic=1.

12. Shyima Hall with Lisa Wysocky, *Hidden Girl: The True Story of a Modern-Day Child Slave* (New York: Simon & Schuster, 2014).

13. US Department of State, "Trafficking in Persons Report," June 2004, http://www.state.gov/documents/organization/34158.pdf.

14. "Charito," interview with the author, July 19, 2010.

15. US Department of Homeland Security, "Eight Arrested on RICO Charges for Visa Fraud, Human Trafficking Conspiracy," news release, May 27, 2009, http://www.ice.gov/news/releases/0905/090527kansascity.htm.

16. "Maria Alvarez," interview with the author, June 21, 2010.

17. Bales and Soodalter, *The Slave Next Door*, 165.

18. "Pocket Assessment Card," Rescue & Restore Campaign Tool Kits, Office of Refugee Resettlement, US Department of Health and Human Services, http://www.acf.hhs.gov/programs/orr/resource/rescue-restore-campaign-tool-kits. Accessed January 13, 2015.

Chapter 5 An Illusion of Pleasure

1. "DEMAND: A Comparative Examination of Sex Tourism and Trafficking in Jamaica, Japan, the Netherlands, and the United States," Shared Hope International, http://sharedhope.org/wp-content/uploads/2012/09/DEMAND.pdf. Accessed January 13, 2015.

2. Catharine A. Mackinnon, "Pornography as Trafficking," in *Pornography: Driving the Demand in International Sex Trafficking*, ed. David E. Guinn and Julie DiCaro (Los Angeles: Captive Daughters Media, 2007).

3. Ibid.

4. Melissa Farley, "'Renting an Organ for Ten Minutes': What Tricks Tell Us about Prostitution, Pornography, and Trafficking," in Guinn and DiCaro, *Pornography*, 5, http://www.prostitutionresearch.com/FarleyRentinganOrgan11-06.pdf.

5. Ibid., 1.

6. Ibid., 2.

7. Seth Lubove, "Sex, Lies and Statistics," *Forbes*, November 23, 2005, http://www.forbes.com/2005/11/22/internet-pornography-children-cz_sl_1123internet.html.

8. Victor Malarek, *The Johns: Sex for Sale and the Men Who Buy It* (New York: Arcade, 2009), 205.

9. McAfee, "The Digital Divide: How the Online Behavior of Teens Is Getting Past Parents," June 30, 2012, http://pornharmsresearch.com/2014/01/mcafee-study-on-parental-involvement-teen-internet-usage/.

10. Office of Refugee Resettlement, "Fact Sheet: Sex Trafficking," August 2, 2012, http://www.acf.hhs.gov/trafficking/about/fact_sex.html.

11. Ibid.

12. Ibid.

13. "H.R.2012: End Demand for Sex Trafficking Act of 2005," Library of Congress, http://thomas.loc.gov/cgi-bin/query/z?c109:H.R.2012:. Accessed January 13, 2015.

14. Shelley Lubben, "Ex-Porn Star Tells the Truth about the Porn Industry," CovenantEyes (blog), October 28, 2008, http://www.covenanteyes.com/2008/10/28/ex-porn-star-tells-the-truth-about-the-porn-industry/.

15. Jersey Jaxin, "Former Porn Star Jersey Jaxin Story," The Pink Cross Foundation, accessed August 9, 2013, https://www.thepinkcross.org/pinkcross-articles/september-2008/former-porn-star-jersey-jaxin-story.

16. Anonymous interview with the author, Febuary 2010.

17. Anonymous interview with the author, February 2010.

18. Ibid.

19. Gail Dines, *Pornland* (Boston: Beacon Press, 2010), 29.

20. Rebecca Carden, "Panel Discusses Human Trafficking, Sex Work in U.S.," *The Brandeis Hoot*, April 23, 2010, http://thebrandeishoot.com/articles/8000.

21. Tony Jones interview with Gail Dines, "Pornland Author Joins *Lateline*," *Lateline*, Australian Broadcasting Corporation, June 10, 2010, http://www.abc.net.au/lateline/content/2010/s3031471.htm.

22. Raymond and Hughes, "Sex Trafficking of Women in the United States."

23. Wendy Kaminer, "Sex-Trafficking, Porn, and the Perils of Legislation," *The Atlantic*, June 9, 2011,http://www.theatlantic.com/national/archive/2011/06/sex-trafficking-porn-and-the-perils-of-legislation/240175/.

24. "Porn Profits: Corporate America's Secret," ABC News, May 27, 2004, http://abcnews.go.com/Primetime/story?id=132370&page=1.

25. Dustin Kass, "Porn Ban: Winona County Adopts 'Clean Hotel' Policy," *Winona Daily News*, September 8, 2010, http://www.winonadailynews.com/news/local/article_b669f574-bb01-11df-87e7-001cc4c002e0.html.

Chapter 6 What's Love Got to Do with It? Absolutely Nothing!

1. Allen testimony, "Domestic Minor Sex Trafficking."

2. Larry Neumeister, "Brothel Raids Expose Problem of Slavery in US," Associated Press, September 3, 2006, http://www.humantrafficking.org/updates/423.

3. Adrienne Sanders, "The City Killed Tiffany Mason: Part 1," *San Francisco Examiner*, May 22, 2002, http://groups.yahoo.com/group/hlf/message/3608.

4. Adrienne Sanders, "Poster Child for Broken Promises: Part 5," *San Francisco Examiner*, May 26, 2002, http://groups.yahoo.com/group/hlf/message/3643.

5. Sanders, "The City Killed Tiffany Mason."

6. Ibid.

7. Adrienne Sanders, "A City Pimp with Big Connections: Part 3," *San Francisco Examiner*, May 22, 2002, http://groups.yahoo.com/group/hlf/message/3607.

8. US Department of Justice, Child Exploitation and Obscenity Section, 2007.

9. Sanders, "The City Killed Tiffany Mason."

10. Ibid.

11. Sanders, "Poster Child for Broken Promises."

12. Ibid.

13. Sanders, "The City Killed Tiffany Mason."

14. Adrienne Sanders, "Pimps Thrive and Girls Die: Part 4," *San Francisco Examiner*, May 24, 2002, http://groups.yahoo.com/group/hlf/message/3632.

15. Sanders, "A City Pimp with Big Connections."

16. Sanders, "Pimps Thrive and Girls Die."

17. Sanders, "Poster Child for Broken Promises."

18. Sanders, "The City Killed Tiffany Mason."

19. Ibid.

20. Sanders, "Poster Child for Broken Promises."

21. Sanders, "Pimps Thrive and Girls Die."

22. Sanders, "Poster Child for Broken Promises."

23. Ibid.

24. Ibid.

25. Ibid.

26. Ibid.

27. Sanders, "Pimps Thrive and Girls Die."

28. Ibid.

29. Ibid.

30. Ibid.

31. Raymond and Hughes, "Sex Trafficking of Women in the United States."

32. Keith Bickford, interview with author, January 14, 2009.

33. Inez, quoted in Kevin Bales and Zoe Trodd, eds., *To Plead Our Own Cause: Personal Stories by Today's Slaves* (Ithaca, NY: Cornell University Press, 2008), 183.

34. Sanders, "The City Killed Tiffany Mason."

35. Sanders, "Poster Child for Broken Promises."

36. Anonymous interview with author.

37. AAP, "Pimps Use Social Media to Lure At-Risk Teens into Prostitution," SBS News, August 29, 2014, http://www.sbs.com.au/news/article/2014/08/29/pimps-use-social-media-lure-risk-teens-prostitution.

38. Jonathan Tran, "Sold into Slavery," *The Christian Century*, November 27, 2008, 22–26.

39. Adrianne Jeffries, "Advocates Want Craigslist to Stop Making Money on 'Adult Services' Ads," September 8, 2010, http://www.readwriteweb.com/archives/advocates_want_craigslist_to_stop_making_money_on.php.

40. Raymond and Hughes, "Sex Trafficking of Women in the United States."

41. Michael B. Farrell, "Global Campaign to Police Child Sex Tourism," *Christian Science Monitor*, April 22, 2004, http://www.csmonitor.com/2004/0422/p11s01-wogi.html.

42. Ibid.

43. Allen testimony, "Domestic Minor Sex Trafficking."

44. Ibid.

45. Anonymous interview with the author, October 2008.

46. Ibid.

47. Anonymous interview with the author, August 20, 2014

48. See for example Evelina Giobbe, "Juvenile Prostitution: Profile of Recruitment" in Ann W. Burgess, ed., *Child Trauma: Issues & Research* (New York: Garland Publishing, 1992); Evelina Giobbe, Mary Harrigan, Jayme Ryan, and

Denise Gamache, *Prostitution: A Matter of Violence against Women* (Minneapolis: Whisper, 1990); and Susan Kay Hunter, "Prostitution Is Cruelty and Abuse to Women and Children," *Michigan Journal of Gender and Law* 1(1994):1–14.

49. Anonymous interview with author, February 2010.

Chapter 7 To the Super Bowl and Beyond

1. Kathleen Madigan, "Number of the Week: How Much Is Super Bowl Really Worth?" *Wall Street Journal*, February 1, 2014, http://blogs.wsj.com/economics/2014/02/01/number-of-the-week-how-much-is-super-bowl-really-worth/.

2. Michael J. Mooney and Gus Garcia-Roberts, "Super Bowl Guide to Sex, Drugs, Gambling, and Living Large in South Florida," *Miami New Times*, February 4, 2010, http://www.miaminewtimes.com/2010-02-04/news/new-times-super-bowl-xliv-guide-to-sex-drugs-gambling-and-living-large-in-south-florida/.

3. Patricia Hynes and Janice G. Raymond, "The Neglected Health Consequences of Sex Trafficking in the United States," in *Policing the National Body: Sex, Race, and Criminalization*, ed. J. Sillman and A. Bhattacharjee (Cambridge, MA: South End, 2002), 1.

4. Dominique Roe-Sepowitz, James Gallagher, and Kristine Hickle, "Exploring Sex Trafficking and Prostitution Demand During the Super Bowl," Arizona State University School of Social Work, March 2014, http://ssw.asu.edu/research/stir/exploring-sex-trafficking-and-prostitution-demand-during-the-super-bowl-2014.

5. Melissa Farley, *Prostitution and Trafficking in Nevada* (San Francisco: Prostitution Research and Education, 2007), 98.

6. US Department of State, "Trafficking in Persons Report," June 2005, http://www.state.gov/documents/organization/47255.pdf.

7. "Teen Girls' Stories of Sex Trafficking in U.S.," ABC News, February 9, 2006, http://abcnews.go.com/Primetime/story?id=1596778&page=1.

8. Vednita Carter and Evelina Giobbe, "Duet: Prostitution, Racism and Feminist Discourse," *Hastings Women's Law Journal* 37 (1999): 46.

9. Quoted in Farley, *Prostitution and Trafficking in Nevada*, 35.

10. *The Today Show*, NBC, December 3, 2008.

11. Anonymous interview with the author, February 2010.

12. Farley, *Prostitution and Trafficking in Nevada*, 181.

13. Ibid., 185.

14. Sam Skolnik, "Do We Have a Human Trafficking Problem?" *Las Vegas Sun*, January 29, 2007,http://www.lasvegassun.com/news/2007/jan/29/do-we-have-a-human-trafficking-problem/.

15. Leslie Bennetts, "The Growing Demand for Prostitution," *Newsweek*, July 18, 2011, http://www.newsweek.com/growing-demand-prostitution-68493.

16. M. Monto and D. Julia, "Conceiving of Sex as a Commodity: A Study of Arrested Customers of Female Street Prostitutes," *Western Criminology Review* 10 (2009), 1–14.

17. Gunilla Ekberg, "The Swedish Law That Prohibits the Purchase of Sexual Services," *Violence Against Women*, October 2004, 1187.

18. "Nearly 500 Sex Buyers Arrested in National Sex Trafficking Sting Operation," Cook County (Illinois) Sheriff's Office, August 6, 2014, http://www

.cookcountysheriff.com/press_page/press_NationalSexTraffickngSting2014_08_06_2014.html.

19. Ib http://www.enddemandillinois.org/sites/default/files/Unlocking_Options_for_Women.pdf.

20. US Department of State, "Trafficking in Persons Report," June 2005, http://www.state.gov/documents/organization/47255.pdf.

21. J. Day, E. Vermilyea, J. Wilkerson, and E. Giller, *Risking Connection in Faith Communities: A Training Curriculum for Faith-Leader Supporting Trauma Survivors* (Baltimore: Sidran Institute Press, 2006).

22. The chart of "Preferred Terminology for Sex Trafficking and Prostitution" originally appeared in L. Thompson, "Introduction to the Global Issue of Human Trafficking" in B. Grant and C. Hudlin, eds., *Hands That Heal: International Curriculum to Train Caregivers of Trafficking Survivors*, academic ed., (Faith Alliance Against Slavery and Trafficking, 2007), 36–40. A revised version of the chart was published in L. Thompson, "Chart of Preferred Terminology for Sex Trafficking and Prostitution," *Social Work & Christianity* 39, no. 4(2012): 484–87.

Chapter 8 Why Victims Stay

1. Uwe Ewald and Ksenija Turković, *Large-Scale Victimization as a Potential Source of Terrorist Activities* (Amsterdam: IOS Press, 2004), 18.

2. The account presented here is drawn from "The Name Is Bond (The Norrmalmstorg Robbery)," narrated by Joe Sinclair, http://www.nurturingpotential.net/Issue13/Name%20is%20Bond.htm.

3. Ibid.

4. Dee L. R. Graham, Edna I. Rawlings, and Roberta K. Rigsby, *Loving to Survive: Sexual Terror, Men's Violence, and Women's Lives* (New York: New York University Press, 1994), 2.

5. Ibid., 1.

6. "The Peace FAQ: The Stockholm Syndrome," http://www.peacefaq.com/stockholm.html.

7. StateMaster.com, s.v. "Norrmalmstorg Robbery," last modified July 2007, http://www.statemaster.com/encyclopedia/Norrmalmstorg-robbery.

8. Graham, Rawlings, and Rigsby, *Loving to Survive*, 10.

9. Ibid., 5.

10. Ibid., 6.

11. Ibid., 7.

12. Ibid.

13. Ibid., 9.

14. Ibid., 10.

15. Ibid.

16. Ibid., 11.

17. Ibid.

18. Joseph M. Carver, "Love and Stockholm Syndrome: The Mystery of Loving an Abuser," *Counseling Resource*, last modified April 27, 2011, http://counsellingresource.com/quizzes/stockholm/.

19. Shawn Hornbeck, "Shawn Hornbeck: Jaycee Dugard Brainwashed, in Shock," *People*, September 4, 2009, http://www.people.com/people/news/category /0„personsTax:ShawnHornbeck,00.html.

20. *New World Encyclopedia*, s.v. "Harriet Tubman," last modified October 30, 2012, http://www.newworldencyclopedia.org/entry/Harriet_Tubman.

21. Raymond and Hughes, "Sex Trafficking of Women in the United States."

22. Farley, *Prostitution and Trafficking in Nevada*, 32.

23. "DSM IV Posttraumatic Stress Disorder: Diagnostic Features," European Society for Traumatic Stress Studies, https://www.estss.org/learn-about-trauma /dsm-iv-ptsd-diagnostic-features/. Accessed January 14, 2015.

24. Rachel Marcus, "Confessions of a Teenage Prostitute," *Portland Mercury*, September 3, 2009, http://www.portlandmercury.com/portland/confessions -of-a-former-teen-rostitute/Content?oid=1623030.

25. Ibid.

26. Ibid.

27. Ibid.

28. Ian Urbina, "For Runaways, Sex Buys Survival," *New York Times*, October 26, 2009, http://www.nytimes.com/2009/10/27/us/27runaways.html?_r=2&hp.

29. "Teen Girls' Stories of Sex Trafficking in the US," ABC News, February 9, 2006, http://abcnews.go.com/Primetime/story?id=1596778.

30. Judith Lewis Herman, *Trauma and Recovery: The Aftermath of Violence—from Domestic Abuse to Political Terror* (New York: Basic Books, 1997), 92–93.

Chapter 9 Wolves in Sheep's Clothing

1. Jody Raphael and Brenda Myers-Powell, "From Victims to Victimizers: Interviews with 25 Ex-Pimps in Chicago," DePaul University College of Law, September 2010, http://newsroom.depaul.edu/pdf/family_law_center_report-final .pdf. Accessed January 14, 2015..

2. "Jason Foster," anonymous interview with the author, April 2010.

3. Girl Scouts of the USA, "Girls and Body Image," n.d., https://www.girlscouts .org/research/pdf/beauty_redefined_factsheet.pdf.

4. "It's Hard out Here for a Pimp," *Wikipedia*, last modified August 12, 2014, http://en.wikipedia.org/wiki/It%27s_Hard_out_Here_for_a_Pimp.

5. "Hidden Slaves: Forced Labor in the United States," a report by Free the Slaves (Washington, DC) and Human Rights Center (University of California at Berkeley), September 2004, http://www.law.berkeley.edu/files/hiddenslaves_report.pdf.

6. Anonymous interview with the author, April 2010

7. "Jason Foster," anonymous interview with the author, April 2010

Chapter 10 On the Front Lines of Modern Slavery

1. Global Forum on Human Trafficking, Carlsbad, CA, October 8, 2009.

2. Keith Bickford, interview with the author, January 14, 2009.

3. Polaris Project, "Human Trafficking Trends in the United States," http:// www.polarisproject.org/resources/hotline-statistics/human-trafficking-trends-in -the-united-states.

4. Quotes and information in this section are derived from interviews with and emails to the author in September 2014.

5. Nicole Moler's quote appears at http://www.truckersagainsttrafficking.org/making-an-impact/.

6. Bales, *Disposable People*, 8.

Appendix: Recognizing the Signs

1. The Polaris Project, "Recognizing the Signs," http://www.polarisproject.org/human-trafficking/recognizing-the-signs. Used by permission.

About the Author

Nita Belles is an author, speaker, and anti–human trafficking crusader who has worked in a broad scope of venues, including victim rescue and restoration, and has served alongside top law enforcement personnel, government officials, social services, and the medical and faith communities to combat human trafficking.

Nita has worked with victims/survivors of human trafficking and also networked with other national and international anti-trafficking organizations. She brings to the table a deep understanding of trafficking with a compassion for victims, a commitment to bring justice to perpetrators, and a determination to link arms with other abolitionists to end modern slavery.

In 2006 Nita began studying about human trafficking. The more she studied, the more she knew she couldn't sit on the sidelines, knowing these atrocities were taking place all over the world, including in her own backyard.

In addition to publishing *In Our Backyard*, Nita has been published in the *Huffington Post*, *Washington Post*, *Journal of Christian Nursing*, and the Billy Graham Evangelistic Association's *Decision Magazine*, among others.

Her work has been featured by CNN and *USA Today* as well as on *FOX Files* and local NBC, CBS, and FOX affiliates, as well as many other media outlets.

After a career in business, Nita earned her master's degree in theology with a concentration in women's concerns. She is a regional director of Oregonians Against Trafficking Humans (OATH) and a member of her local Human Trafficking Task Force.

Nita directs a team that works with law enforcement, nonprofits, social services, and other government officials to help bring justice to perpetrators and the best of services to recovered victims. Her levelheaded approach brings to the table years of Super Bowl experience and many networking resources.

Nita is a sought-after trainer and motivational speaker, having presented to law enforcement, attorneys general, universities, civic organizations, medical communities, conferences, and faith-based groups. Some of her specific venues include National Association of Attorneys General, Oregon Youth Authority Parole and Probation, Saddleback Church, Willow Creek Church, and multiple universities and colleges. She instructs from experience, having worked with victims from rescue to restoration. She is committed to staying current by working in "boots on the ground" operations. As a result of many years of anti–domestic violence work, she has a deep understanding of the dynamics of both victims and perpetrators.

In her business career, Nita started, built, and sold a successful printing business. Additionally, she has worked as an associate pastor and domestic violence chaplain.

Nita is available to present to groups everywhere, whether offering specific trainings or simply bringing awareness. She has an enthusiasm for life and is known as a powerful motivator who will impact any group to which she has the opportunity to present.

**HUMAN TRAFFICKING
IN OUR BACKYARD**

JOIN THE MOVEMENT

LINKING ARMS ACROSS AMERICA IN THE FIGHT AGAINST HUMAN TRAFFICKING

www.InOurBackyard365.org